ISSUES THAT CONCERN YOU

Choosing a College

Norah Piehl, *Book Editor*

GREENHAVEN PRESS
A part of Gale, Cengage Learning

GALE
CENGAGE Learning™

Detroit • New York • San Francisco • New Haven, Conn • Waterville, Maine • London

Elizabeth Des Chenes, *Managing Editor*

Articles in Greenhaven Press anthologies are often edited for length to meet page require-ments. In addition, original titles of these works are changed to clearly present the main thesis and to explicitly indicate the author's opinion. Every effort is made to ensure that Greenhaven Press accurately reflects the original intent of the authors. Every effort has been made to trace the owners of copyrighted material.

Cover image Copyright © Supri Suharjoto/Shutterstock.com.

LIBRARY OF CONGRESS CATALOGING-IN-PUBLICATION DATA

Choosing a college / Norah Piehl, book editor.
    p. cm. -- (Issues that concern you)
  Includes bibliographical references and index.
  ISBN 978-0-7377-5691-3 (hardback)
 1. College choice--United States--Juvenile literature. 2. Universities and colleges--United States--Admission--Juvenile literature. I. Piehl, Norah.
  LB2350.5.C58 2012
  378.1'980973--dc23

2011051626

Printed in the United States of America
2 3 4 5 6 7 16 15 14 13 12

CONTENTS

In early 2010, 180 students visited the campus of the University of California at Merced. They toured classroom buildings, talked to current students, and ate lunch in the dining hall. This might sound like a typical college open house, the kind of event colleges and universities nationwide host for high school juniors and seniors each year. In this case, however, the visiting students still had years—not months—before they would apply to college. These visiting students were sixth graders at a local middle school, participants in a US Department of Education initiative called "GEAR UP" (Gaining Early Awareness and Readiness for Undergraduate Programs). This program aims to get young students—and their parents—interested in college and eager to make the most of their high school years with the goal of college in sight. The students that GEAR UP aims to help are low-income students, those who would become the very first in their family to attend college. GEAR UP's organizers hope that by taking young students *to* college, those students might picture themselves *in* college. In California fewer than 20 percent of low-income students who start high school have completed a higher education degree ten years later. Perhaps early exposure to the exciting, appealing college environment can help reduce that trend among lower-income students.

For many students in higher-income families, there is little question as to whether they will attend college. The focus, rather, is on how to get in and how to pay for it. Middle class parents are often advised—rightly so, given the skyrocketing rates of college tuition and fee inflation—to start saving for college when their children are babies, if not before. The planning goes beyond the financial aspect, however, as explained by college guidance counselor Avis Wright in an article at the website of Northwestern University's Center for Talent Development. She advises middle school students and their parents to pay attention to dozens of details, from developing good study skills to enrolling in accelerated courses to participating in challenging extracurricular activities. In answer to the question of whether middle school is too early to start planning for college, Wright answers, "It may be too late!" The Baltimore Public School system apparently agrees with Wright; they sponsor an art and essay contest with the theme "What College Means to Me," open to students as young as kindergarten.

But what does college really mean to a child in kindergarten, or even in middle school? For many younger students, the future is a place for undefined hopes and dreams; their career aspirations might include becoming a pro athlete, an astronaut, a ballerina, or a fire fighter. In *Head Start to College Planning*, Susan Chiarolanzio advises that "beginning the college search too

Because of rapidly escalating college costs, experts recommend that parents begin saving for college while their children are infants.

early will result in wasted effort as the factors to consider cannot be clearly defined or may be erroneous if the child is still too young to know what he wants." For parents tracking monthly contributions to their child's college savings account, the college years can seem frighteningly close, but for many younger students, college still seems like a distant dream, an undefined component of "when I grow up."

Although parents can certainly help create a nurturing, supportive environment in which academic excellence is encouraged and ambitious goals are explored, and although there are certainly very real timetables dictated by factors such as standardized testing and application deadlines, some advisers suggest that perhaps the best plan is to let students take the lead for their own college planning readiness.

The question of when and how to start the process of choosing a college is just one of the issues that students face today. Authors in *Issues That Concern You: Choosing a College* examine many issues, including entrance exams, admissions essays, and dealing with rejection. In addition, the volume contains several appendixes to help the reader understand and explore the topic, including a thorough bibliography and a list of organizations to contact for further information. The appendix titled "What You Should Know About Choosing a College" includes information about how to identify your interests and offers criteria for evaluating colleges. The appendix "What You Should Do About Choosing a College" offers tips for the college search, including how to get organized and where to seek help. With all of these features, *Issues That Concern You: Choosing a College* provides a thorough resource for everyone interested in this issue.

ONE

SAT Scores Are One of Many Factors Considered by Admissions Counselors

John Andrew Williams

During the stressful process of applying for colleges, it can be easy to lose sight of the big picture. Part of the important process of gaining perspective, according to John Andrew Williams, is remembering that standardized test scores are only one of many criteria that admissions counselors consider. In this article Williams offers suggestions for students whose SAT scores might not have lived up to their own expectations and for those whose test scores seem out of balance with the rest of their admissions package. His advice is intended to encourage even the most test-phobic students.

Williams's mission in life is to revolutionize education. He is a certified life coach and college consultant and the founder of the college-consulting firm Top Ten Skills and Academic Life Coaching. Williams is the author of *Future-Proofed: Your Guide to Acing High School, the College Application, and Beyond*.

E ven if you don't nail the SATs, you can still tailor your application to make your positive attributes stand out.

What can you do to overcome lousy SAT scores on your college application?

Relax, and take a deep breath. The SAT is only a slice of your application. Sure, it's important, and a high score can certainly open some campus doors, but don't forget that there are many other factors that comprise your college profile: your GPA, application essays, teacher recommendations, and a campus interview.

College admissions departments generally consider SAT scores as just one aspect of a students' application; other factors, such as grade point average and application essays, are also considered.

What's more, there's a small but growing trend among college admissions offices today to dispense with SAT scores altogether. Top-tier schools like Bates College, Bowdoin, College of the Holy Cross, Smith College, and Wake Forest University are just a few of the schools that have decided to make SAT scores optional. . . .

Most selective colleges use SAT scores not as a formulaic cutoff to weed out students, but simply as a guide or another piece of information to give the admissions office a larger picture of the applicant. If you have a stellar transcript and worthwhile extracurricular activities, your SAT scores should not hold you back from finding a rigorous college. And remember, the SAT is just one part of your application. If your score is not where you want it to be, take a deep breath, and push on. You'll do fine.

Tips for Success

Here are a few tips on how to tailor your application so you have the best chance for success:

1. Write the college essay you were going to write—without excuses like "I don't test well."

Your college essay should be where the college admissions officers get to know you as a person and discover your passions and the value you would bring to the university. Excuses or explaining why you didn't do better on the SAT in your main application essay will just draw attention to your low score!

2. Your high-school guidance counselor can weigh in.

If there is a legitimate reason why your test didn't go well, a letter of recommendation from a guidance counselor is a good place for that explanation.

3. If there's an optional essay [as] part of the application, write it!

Some colleges have an optional essay. If you have a low SAT score, take the opportunity to explain why this happened, but be careful not to come across as whiny. Still, a strong essay can go a long way to augment an application.

4. Apply to reach schools: don't rule any out based on an SAT score.

I've seen students rejected at local state schools but admitted to Ivy League colleges because the state schools used a formula to determine a student's eligibility while the Ivies, in this case Dartmouth and Brown, looked at the whole picture of a student. Remember to check out schools that don't require you to report your SAT scores. . . . SAT-optional schools sometimes create surprising results. One student I worked with was rejected from the University of Oregon but accepted to Sarah Lawrence. (He's a junior now at Sarah Lawrence and pulling in straight A's.)

Of course, having a good SAT score definitely helps your admission odds and your chances of earning merit scholarships, but a low one doesn't mean you're doomed. Still, it's worthwhile to put the time and energy into studying for the SAT so you can improve your score.

5. *Take the SAT more than once.*

No matter what your score is the first time you take the SAT, it's a good idea to take the test again. It probably won't hurt, since most schools will take the highest score from each section. And often students do better the second time around because they are more familiar with the test. Ideally, you would take the test in the spring of your junior year and then again in the fall of your senior year. Colleges will usually look at your combined highest score. For instance, let's say the first time you take the test you do well in the math section but don't do as well in the reading and writing portions. When you prepare to take the test again, focus on practicing reading and writing. If your scores are higher the second time around in those sections, colleges will usually put those together with your high math score from the first time you took the test.

6. *Study consistently for the test.*

I've seen the best improvement in SAT scores from students who spend about an hour or more each week taking practice tests and then consistently going over concepts and vocabulary they need to learn. I've found that students who set aside the same time each week to study have the best success. For instance, Sunday nights from 8 to 9 p.m. is a popular time to do SAT preparation.

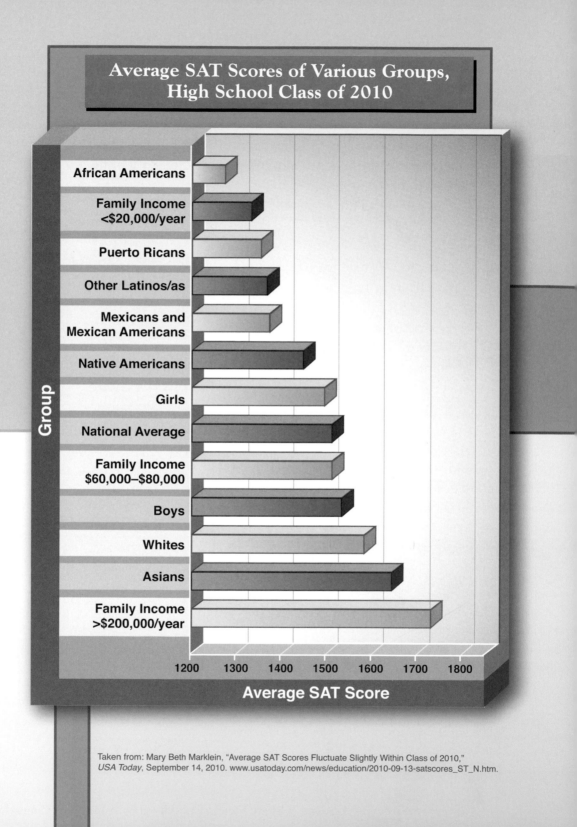

Average SAT Scores of Various Groups, High School Class of 2010

Group

- African Americans
- Family Income <$20,000/year
- Puerto Ricans
- Other Latinos/as
- Mexicans and Mexican Americans
- Native Americans
- Girls
- National Average
- Family Income $60,000–$80,000
- Boys
- Whites
- Asians
- Family Income >$200,000/year

1200 1300 1400 1500 1600 1700 1800

Average SAT Score

Taken from: Mary Beth Marklein, "Average SAT Scores Fluctuate Slightly Within Class of 2010," *USA Today*, September 14, 2010. www.usatoday.com/news/education/2010-09-13-satscores_ST_N.htm.

7. Use online resources.

Many students sign up for an SAT prep class, which is a good idea if you want to spend the money. But there's also plenty of information available on the Web. Several Web sites have free practice tests and tips. The best places to start are the College Board (www.collegeboard.com/) and Princeton Review (www.princeton review.com/college/sat-psat-practice.aspx). Both sites offer full-length practice tests.

TWO

College Fairs Provide Important Information

Natalia Maldonado

College fairs can be an important early step in the college application process, but they can also be overwhelming. In this article Natalia Maldonado offers high school students important suggestions to minimize time-wasting and to maximize usefulness. She suggests approaching the college fair as an information-gathering exercise, one that should help answer questions and narrow down the huge field of potential school choices. Maldonado offers several concrete, practical suggestions for even the youngest students just starting their college search process.

After graduating from the University of Miami with a degree in creative writing and a minor in journalism, Maldonado worked as an editor at a start-up publication in Miami Beach until Maldonado recognized that writing was her true passion. She specializes in interviews and profiles as well as articles on arts, culture, health, and wellness.

Being choosy is not always a bad thing, especially when it comes to picking the right college. The process can seem overwhelming. But a trip to a college fair can help you narrow your choices.

"A college fair is a place where colleges come to answer questions and give out information," says Angel Woodward, a career counselor at the Jefferson County School District in Kentucky. "College representatives talk to students personally about what they can expect at their institution or location."

Whether held in a conference room, school gym, or convention center, most fairs include a huge range of colleges, each with a booth where admissions counselors answer students' questions. The one-on-one interaction can give you insight you might not find on a school's Web site, but a large college fair can also feel like a web of its own. The trick to navigating it is research.

"It's important for students to be prepared because college fairs can be a great way for them to connect with a college representative who could advocate for them if they decide to apply to that school," says Steve Pinto, associate director of admissions at Dickinson College in Carlisle, Pa. "Admissions counselors are eager to share information about their institutions, so students should come prepared with good questions and some idea of the type of schools they are looking for."

Know Before You Go

There may be hundreds of colleges at the fair. Review the list of schools ahead of time and note which ones you've researched, discussed with your school counselor, and have some interest in. "Visit those schools first," suggests Pinto. "Most students start in row one and ask vague questions and take brochures and run out of time to get to the schools they really want to see."

Tyler Peters, a junior at Coral Gables Senior High School in Miami, made a list of 10 colleges he wanted to look into before attending the 2008 Miami National College Fair. They ranged from state schools, such as the University of Florida and Florida State University, which he knew offer scholarships to in-state residents, to out-of-state schools, including Michigan State University.

Tyler and his mom, Adrienne Peters, went over a map of the fair that showed the locations of the colleges in attendance, and circled the ones on their list. "She's the master chief," Tyler joked as his mom navigated their way through the crowd.

Along the way, they ran into some of Tyler's classmates. Some were at the fair with friends; others were on their own.

The author stresses that prospective students should prepare for college fairs by researching the schools that interest them and being ready to ask focused questions of those colleges' representatives.

Both ways can make for different experiences, says Linda Kimmel, college and career center adviser at Irvington High School in Fremont, Calif. "I've noticed students are more open to asking questions if they're with their peers," she says. "So while I think parents should go, I think it's helpful if the students ask the questions on their own and not depend on the parents to ask for them."

Questions and Answers

As they moved through the fair gathering brochures and information cards, Tyler took a few minutes to speak with each representative. Think of this time as a small interview, in which you ask the questions. The best questions are the ones tailored specifically to your needs. "What is your swimming program like?" Tyler asked a representative from Michigan State. Because he is on his high school swim team, he asked about athletic scholarships as well as scholarships offered for academics. He also wanted to know what Michigan State was looking for in a student.

"Questions I like to hear from students are those whose answers cannot be found in a brochure or fact sheet," says Pinto. While there's nothing wrong with asking questions about class size and average SAT scores, he says, "students should also ask questions about the vision and defining characteristics of the college." Then students can better determine if the school is a good match to their goals.

Make Contact

Many college representatives had Tyler fill out a contact card so they could send him more information on the programs he was interested in. Be prepared to fill out a lot of these cards as you go from booth to booth. To make the most of your time, bring along printed adhesive labels with your demographic information on them: name, address, e-mail address, phone number, grade-point average, any majors you're interested in, and when you're graduating. "When students come to the tables, they just take the label and stick it on the contact card, and they can move much more efficiently through the fair," says Jennifer Schufer, associate director for student recruitment at the University of Colorado at Boulder.

Some fairs are finding new ways to make information gathering faster. At the 2008 Miami National College Fair, sponsored by the National Association for College Admission Counseling, Tyler was asked to enter his information into a computer. Then he received a printout with a bar code that linked to all his contact information. As Tyler went from one college booth to another, representatives scanned his information into their systems instead of having him fill out cards.

Away from the individual colleges, special sessions at a college fair provide information on topics such as applying for financial aid, writing a college essay, taking the SAT and ACT, and college preparation for ninth and 10th graders. Each session is offered repeatedly throughout a college fair, so you can attend these in between exploring the colleges' booths.

Take Your Pick

By the end of a college fair, you should have a good idea of which colleges you like and even a few you plan on applying to. After visiting six booths, including New College of Florida, Boston University, Tulane University, the University of Colorado at Boulder, and the United States Air Force Academy, Tyler was considering applying to about five colleges. "I'm definitely going to apply to the University of Florida and Florida State because of Bright Futures [a state-funded scholarship for students who meet certain grade requirements]," he said. "I'll apply to Colorado at Boulder. I had a great experience at that table, though I hadn't been considering it at first. A school like Boulder captures a lot of my interests. I know that they have a really, really great swimming program, and the representative was very friendly." A photographic map that stretched across the table also helped Tyler visualize the campus. "A lot of places don't have that, all you see is their name." He took note of important dates, such as application deadlines, in a small notebook he carried in his pocket, and he had a bag full of brochures and business cards to take home.

Even if you're not close to the application process, it's never too early to go to a college fair. While most attendees are in their junior or senior year, sophomores, freshmen, and even junior high students can get a lot from the experience. Attending college fairs "allows them to begin to see the options that are out there so that they can make better decisions when it's time to make them," says Woodward.

Knowing what grade point averages and standardized test scores colleges are expecting can help students set goals throughout high school. "Just going and selecting two campuses to get materials from will . . . broaden their of idea of why they need to be serious in junior high and high school," Schufer says.

Most Students Focus Applications on a Few Colleges

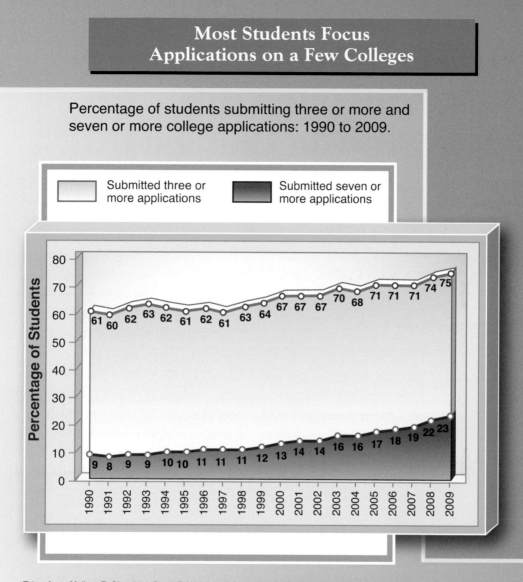

Percentage of students submitting three or more and seven or more college applications: 1990 to 2009.

Submitted three or more applications

Submitted seven or more applications

Percentage of Students

Three or more: 61, 60, 62, 63, 62, 61, 62, 61, 63, 64, 67, 67, 67, 70, 68, 71, 71, 71, 74, 75

Seven or more: 9, 8, 9, 9, 10, 10, 11, 11, 11, 12, 13, 14, 14, 16, 16, 17, 18, 19, 22, 23

Years: 1990 1991 1992 1993 1994 1995 1996 1997 1998 1999 2000 2001 2002 2003 2004 2005 2006 2007 2008 2009

Taken from: Melissa E. Clinedinst, Sarah F. Hurley, and David A. Hawkins, "2010 State of College Admissions," National Association for College Admission Counseling, 2010. www.nacacnet.org/PublicationsResources/Research/Documents/2011SOCA.pdf.

So bring a bag, pens, preprinted labels, good questions, and an open mind. The right school for you might be just a few tables down the row.

THREE

Campus Visits Provide Previews of College Life

Jessica King

Even with all the resources and information available online, there is still no replacement for an in-person campus visit. In this article Jessica King offers students suggestions for ways to make the most of their college visits. These include down-to-earth considerations (make sure you've made reservations) and more high-level ones (visit a college when school is actually in session). With these suggestions in hand, King says, prospective students should find the campus visit not only an important fact-finding mission but also an enjoyable "dry run" for college life.

King is a contributing editor for *Careers & Colleges* magazine.

Choosing a college is a huge investment—for your future and your bank account. It's important that you take the right steps to ensure that the college you decide on is the right fit. A great tool of evaluation is the campus visit. You might wonder: with all the benefits that a technologically savvy society has to offer, is a campus visit really necessary? Definitely. A campus visit allows you to gain a feel for the atmosphere of your prospective college and will help you in your decision-making process. Here are a few tips to help you prepare for your visit.

Proper Planning Is Key

Plan ahead. Call the admission office to find out when tours and information sessions are offered. Do a little research about the school so you can prove you are well prepared and knowledgeable. Ask if you can speak with a current student, professor in your intended field of study, a coach, an admission officer, or a financial aid officer (they can answer the difficult questions about paying for your education). Most campuses require reservations, so plan accordingly!

Take your time. Allow at least half a day for each campus visit. This gives you enough time to interview, tour, and explore all you need. Any less, and you won't gain a full understanding of what the college has to offer. Map out routes and schedules ahead of time to make sure you are making the most of your visit.

Dress appropriately. The first impression is important. You may meet an admission counselor or go for an interview, so it is important to dress neatly and properly. Also, you may want to wear comfortable shoes because you'll be walking a lot. Finally, plan for the weather.

Get the Full Experience

Try it out. Eat lunch in the dining hall. Sit in on a class. Catch a football or soccer game. The best way to answer your questions about a college is to go find out for yourself. Why ask a tour guide if the food is any good when you can grab a snack from the dining hall and taste it for yourself? Firsthand experience is a great way to discover if you like the atmosphere of a college and a major benefit of a campus visit, so take advantage of it!

Visit while school's in. Summer may be the most convenient time to visit a campus, but it's not the best. Often campuses are deserted because most students are home for summer break. The same is true for winter and spring breaks. Also, avoid exam time. The atmosphere provided by stressed-out students hunkered down in the library is not typical of the rest of the year. And finally, major campus events such as commencement, homecoming, or opening weekend of the fall semester may prove to

Making the Most of a Campus Visit

Common questions you should always ask:

• Ask what the transition is like from from high school to college.

• Ask about the food, residence halls, and class sizes.

• Ask about campus safety.

Questions you should ask, but sometimes don't:

• Ask about the tour guide's personal experience at the school.

• Ask why the tour guide chose the school.

• Ask the tour guide what they would change about the school.

• Ask about the academic and career services available to students.

Taken from: Rebecca Kern, "Questions to Ask on College Campus Tours," US News.com, April 2, 2010. www.usnews.com/education/best-colleges/right-school/tours/articles/2010/04/02/questions-to-ask-on-college-campus-tours.

be too busy to get the attention that you deserve. To get the most out of your campus visit, try to visit during the middle of the fall or spring semester, while campuses are humming with activity and you can get the full campus effect.

Stay overnight. It's the best way to imagine you are a student. By spending a night in the dorms, you can gain a viewpoint on what life would really be like if you attended that college. Some colleges allow prospective students to spend a night with a current student in a dorm. If this is impossible due to limited space or unavailability, then talk to your guidance counselor. Graduates from your high school may be glad to host a student for a night. Even if you can't arrange an overnight stay, you still want to check out the dorms. After all, you'll spend most of your time in your room, so you want to make sure you are comfortable there.

Visit the city. When you visit a campus, you want to make sure you check out its surroundings. Make sure that if you need something, the city or town the campus is in can provide it. Check out the local restaurants, parks, and museums. Will you need a car, or is there easy and available public transportation? During all the excitement of a campus visit, don't forget you are going to be living there for the next few years. Make sure everything you need is at hand.

Prospective students and their parents tour Bowdoin College in Maine. Visits to specific campuses can be key in determining which college is best suited to an individual.

Pick up a newspaper. Student newspapers are one of the best sources for finding out what campus life is like. Look up what activities are happening or what the articles focus on. Newspapers can really show what's important to the student body. Bulletin boards can give you the same type of information as well, so keep your eyes open during your tour of the campus!

Get involved. Actually talk to students. They can provide great inside information that you may not find on a website or in a brochure. Ask them what they love about the school and what they are not so fond of. Prepare important questions ahead of time and find someone who can answer them for you. Another great way to gain information from a campus visit is through a group information session. Others may have questions that didn't occur to you. In general, the students have a lot of information to give you if you just ask, so don't be shy.

Evaluate Your Experience

Reflect. Take notes. You are going to be visiting a lot of campuses (hopefully), and you are going to need those notes to remember and make comparisons. If it's possible, take pictures of points of interest to remind you what the campus was like. When you get home, send thank you notes or e-mails to interviewers and admission officials who helped you along the way. Then begin to compare the schools. Figure out what you liked about them and what you hated. Picture yourself as a student at each campus and try to discover which seems the best fit. With a bit of luck and some preparation, your campus visits will help you choose the right school for you.

FOUR

College Rankings Are Overrated

Philadelphia Inquirer Editorial Staff

> For years, both prospective college students and college administrators have scoured the annual college rankings published by *US News & World Report*, checking out how they, or their choices, stack up against the competition. In this editorial originally published in the *Philadelphia Inquirer*, the editors point out that several of the criteria utilized by the rankings are statistically questionable and are too often manipulated by colleges and universities interested in padding their rankings at the expense of actually investing in improving their programs. The editors advise high school students to broaden their outlook beyond the numerical rankings, to establish their own criteria, and do more substantial research into colleges across the ratings spectrum.
>
> The *Philadelphia Inquirer* is a daily newspaper founded in 1829.

Americans, pressed for time and eager for dish, love lists.

Not surprisingly, well-known people or institutions that fare badly on well-known lists tend to be less fond of them.

So, at first blush, you might think sour grapes was on the menu this week as a gathering of college presidents blasted the influential *U.S. News & World Report* rankings of "America's Best Colleges."

But wait. The Annapolis Group, the association of liberal arts colleges that just pledged to help develop a better alternative to the *U.S. News* list, includes every one of the colleges in the magazine's Top 10 national liberal arts colleges. That list includes Swarthmore (No. 3) and Haverford (No. 9).

Perhaps something else was driving the agitation at the group's meeting next to Chesapeake Bay.

It's this: *U.S. News'* clout in determining perceptions of academic value on campus has gotten out of hand. Even allowing for educators' typical reluctance to be judged by outsiders, the college presidents are right to seek to wriggle free.

The rankings are a good idea gone malignant. They've taken on far more meaning than any arbitrary statistical formula should. They have become a prime factor in the college admissions "arms race," which makes parents of smart kids behave like crazy people and often makes those wonderful kids feel like losers at age 17 because they "only" got into Muhlenberg, not Amherst; "only" into Penn State, not Brown.

The nonsense has hit dreadful proportions. It does the cause of genuine education no good and should be curbed.

Of course, colleges and their presidents have been largely complicit in this spiral into nuttiness. In 1983, *U.S. News* began its rankings, betting correctly that parents of college-age kids would hail any bid to give them understandable, consumer-oriented information about the dark, costly mysteries of higher ed. It's likely that about eight seconds after the first rankings came out, the first college sent out a press release bragging about its rating.

The ratings, tweaked and refined over the years, combine various measures of a college's attributes and appeal, from average class size, to percentage of alumni who give, to percentage of applicants accepted, to percentage of accepted applicants who decide to attend ("yield").

All of the measures are plausible, but no number can really measure the heart of the question, the quality of the learning, scholarship and socialization that happen on a given campus.

Bob Morse (pictured) runs US News & World Report's *annual rankings of top colleges. Critics say the ranking system is arbitrary and undeserving of its prestigious reputation.*

To be fair, *U.S. News* doesn't oversell the validity of its rankings; but it doesn't lament the outsized importance they've come to exercise. After all, that has turned the rankings into a lucrative product line.

The rankings also include, and heavily weight, the results of surveys of college presidents about their perception of the quality of other institutions.

A majority of the 80 college presidents at the Annapolis Group session last week vowed to stop taking part in that very

US News & World Report Top-Ranked National Universities, 2011

| 1. Harvard University |
| 2. Princeton University |
| 3. Yale University |
| 4. Columbia University |
| 5. Stanford University |
| 6. University of Pennsylvania |
| 7. California Institute of Technology |
| 8. Massachusetts Institute of Technology |
| 9. Dartmouth College |
| 10. Duke University |

Taken from: *US News & World Report*, "National University Rankings," 2011.
http://colleges.usnews.rankingsandreviews.com/best-colleges/ranking/national-universities.

subjective beauty contest, which tends to cement the position of certain prestigious brand-name colleges and to undervalue excellent but lesser-known colleges.

Fact is, the prestige of a college is no guarantee that it will match up with the needs, personality and aspirations of a given student. Lots of students get mediocre educations at "good" schools, while others learn tremendously at lesser-known schools.

What's more disturbing, the rankings have become an end in themselves in higher education. Alumni and trustees fret over their school's rating. Administrators have been known to get bonuses for pushing their schools up the rankings. And this has led to no end of gambits to game the magazine's rating system, sometimes with damaging results for families.

Examples:

One way to increase yield, the percentage of a college's acceptances who actually matriculate, is to boost the percentage of students you accept "early decision." This trend to binding decisions in the fall of senior year has stampeded many students into the wrong school, and undercut many families' bargaining position on aid.

To increase "selectivity" (i.e. lowering the percentage of applicants accepted) some colleges indulge in P.R. campaigns to persuade students with little chance of being accepted to go through the trouble and expense of applying.

Average SAT scores of entering classes remain a factor in the formula. This can't help the acceptance chances of quirky, creative kids whose talents may not be well-measured by standardized tests.

Finally, the whole prestige chase, fueled by *U.S. News*, enables elite colleges to raise tuitions at rates outstripping inflation and seemingly immune to market pressure.

So, OK, the *U.S. News* rankings have gotten out of control. But the enterprise became a cottage industry for a reason. Parents and students thirst for an accessible, organized, thorough source of comparative information on colleges.

Actually, a host of fat books you can find at your local bookstore do a pretty good, qualitative job of that. But at-a-glance charts chock-full of statistics do have value. Recognizing that, the Annapolis Group presidents have agreed to work with the National Association of Independent Colleges and Universities and the Council of Independent Colleges to develop a better alternative to *U.S. News*.

The burden is on them to produce. Pick up those No. 2 pencils and get to work, folks.

FIVE

Paid Admissions Consultants Can Be Useful

Charles Paikert

As Charles Paikert points out in this article, business is booming for the recently developed field of college admissions consulting or advising. The parents of college-bound high school students often pay thousands of dollars for these consultants' services. These consultants' background and expertise, however, can vary widely. Paikert's focus here is on advisers who offer students and their parents an important type of analysis: matching up not only a student's aptitudes and interests with a prospective school but also a family's ability to pay with the prospective school's likely financial package. Certified financial advisers can also help families plan how to pay for the college of their choice.

Paikert is the editor of Registered Rep's *Wealth Management Letter,* a website for financial advisers. He has previously been the editor of *Family Wealth Report* and has contributed articles for *Investment News,* the *New York Times, Barron's,* Reuters, the *Nation,* and the *Washington Post,* among other publications. His specialties include business and investment issues.

Financial adviser Letha Costin has spent several weeks this year doing something most other advisers don't: She has been working with a dozen college-bound 11th-graders in Raleigh, N.C., on the admissions process.

Using software from ApplyWise LLC, Ms. Costin helps find the right college for each teen and prepares them for admission through three to six personalized coaching sessions, for which she charges $95 an hour.

Response to the business has been "excellent," according to Ms. Costin, who added the coaching service a year ago [2007] to Raleigh-based Innovative Advisors, the firm she runs with her husband, Miles Costin. "We're seeing a big demand for this kind of service," she said.

Brisk Business

Business is also brisk for College and Retirement Solutions LLC in Chatham, N.J., which works with families on the admissions process.

"We've seen admissions becoming significantly more important for families over the last two years," said Nancy Ziering, president of the firm.

"There have been a record number of students applying for college, and colleges are giving less financial aid," she said. "We help clients find schools that will reward students based on their achievements so the cost can be affordable."

"If done properly, admissions work can be a very useful tool," Ms. Ziering added. "We try to educate parents so they don't pick a school just because their child wants to go there. They have to understand what schools are looking for so they match their child to the right school to create leverage."

High Demand

According to Liz Hamburg, chief operating officer of ApplyWise of New York, several advisers a week from all over the country are signing up to use her web-based software about the college admissions process.

"I don't have specific numbers on how many advisers are currently using ApplyWise," she said, "but it has been growing rapidly.

A mother and her son confer with a paid admissions consultant (left) about college admissions procedures.

Many advisers have begun to offer some form of admissions advising in addition to financial planning. Advisers are hearing the same questions over and over again about where to apply and how to apply. There's a demand for expert advice."

Advisers and planners don't necessarily have to be experts in college admissions, said Troy Onink, co-author with Lloyd Paradiso of *Strategy and Simplicity for Private School and College Funding*. . . . The book includes a chapter on refining the school search.

Financial Advice

Still, Mr. Onink believes that advisers would be "well-served to provide some information about affordability and the right fit for a student."

Advisers should be able to help guide parents to schools that are "within an affordable price range," he continued, "with the understanding that many private colleges have the ability to provide the student with aid that in the end may make the cost of a private school the same as a public school."

Others think advisers should stick to financial planning.

"There's a lot of great information about college admissions that's easily available," said Peter Miralles, Dunwoody, Ga.–based president of Atlanta Wealth Consultants LLC. "Planning is where I can help my clients."

"Planners should be involved in how to pay for college, not evaluate which colleges to pay for," said Peter Mazareas, vice chairman of the Washington-based College Savings Foundation and chief executive of Nahant, Mass.–based Strategic Advancement Group Inc.

But according to Mr. Costin, who concentrates on college funding as well as financial retirement planning at Innovative Advisers, clients who receive admissions coaching from his wife "are more likely to hear what I have to say, and take the next step."

SIX

Admissions Essays Are Not Always the Work of the Applicant

Julia Reischel

In this article Julia Reischel profiles the people—mostly recent Ivy League graduates—who are in the business of editing admissions essays. The ethical foundations of the firms who employ these writers are open to debate. Some say the services they provide level the playing field for students who struggle with writing. Others say the services amount to plagiarism. Surprisingly, many colleges tolerate or even support essay-editing services, arguing that the essay is just one component of a multi-faceted admissions package. As the availability of these services increases, these questions will continue to gain importance.

Reischel is the editor and publisher of the *Watershed Post*, an online newspaper that covers news, arts, culture, and the environment in New York City's watershed. Her work has also appeared in *Lawyers Weekly*, the *Village Voice*, and the *Boston Phoenix*, among other publications.

It's December, the height of college application season, and students across Massachusetts are hunched over their desks, putting the finishing touches on their college application essay. Traditionally, that essay has been viewed as a chance to break loose from the drone of dry figures and bullet points, and get to a place where unadulterated personality and a compelling story are enough to put a hopeful over the top. Or at least that was the case when students were still writing their own essays, which, increasingly, they aren't.

So let's start over.

The Rise of Editing Services

It's December, the height of college application season, and hundreds of anonymous Ivy League graduates are hunched over their desks, putting a shine on the personal statements of kids they've never met face-to-face, practicing their craft over the Internet, and for good money. Last year [2007] was the most competitive admissions season in history, and these freelance editors, and the multiplying number of firms they work for, are doing a booming business in this latest extension of what has come to be known as the "admissions industrial complex." In an age in which SAT scores can be bumped up by buying a thousand-dollar test-prep course and parents will pay private academic counselors tens of thousands of dollars to help brand their kids for colleges, it should come as little surprise that there's also a thriving trade in "perfect" application essays.

"It's become a big industry," says Chuck Hughes, cofounder of Road to College, a local admissions-consulting firm. Essay editing is just one of the services his company offers, but there are at least a dozen operations out there that do enough business in essay editing to make it their primary focus. The biggest, and a pioneer of the field, is EssayEdge: Now headquartered in New Jersey, it got its start in Cambridge, where it was founded in a Harvard dorm room in 1997. Several others are based locally [near Braton], including All Ivy Educational Services, founded this spring [2007] in a Somerville apartment, and Cambridge Coaching, which is staffed by grad students at Harvard and MIT. The Writing Center, started by 2006 Harvard grad Nathan Labenz as a way to fund a year of travel abroad, was based here last summer, when Labenz was in town living with friends. "I'm just picking up the crumbs," Labenz says. "I think this stuff is only getting crazier, partly because the Internet is making it easier."

As the industry grows, however, so do concerns that these services, if not explicitly promoting plagiarism, at the very least run counter to the central mission of higher education. After all, helping students fake or exaggerate learning in order to gain

The bane of every college applicant: the admissions essay.

access to more learning seems a little dubious. But some essay editors argue that such criticism is a bit . . . academic. What they're doing, they claim, is merely responding to market pressure. "If clients are going to pay me a fortune to get into the system," says one editor at the Writing Center, "I'm happy to reap the benefits."

How It Works

It works like this: For fees of $60 and (way) up, essay-editing services turn rough drafts, outlines, and even raw biographical information into finished masterpieces suitable for submitting straight to the admissions office. EssayEdge's guidelines for its editors tell them to make clients' essays "substantially better": "If the average essay we see is a C, you should return at least a B+/A-. . . . The edited essay should be compelling and not just slightly improved. . . . Cut, add, reorganize at will." Another company, GradeSaver, tells its potential editors to "imagine this is your college application essay" and "make every necessary change to make this essay the best it can be."

The essay editors who take on the job do so for the obvious reason: money. Hapless humanities majors fresh out of elite schools line up to work for these editing services, which themselves have acceptance rates on par with those of top-ranking colleges. (EssayEdge boasts that it rejects 50 applicants for every one hired.) Once they're in, editors can earn anywhere from $40 to $100 per essay, plus bonuses ranging from $10 to $50 per happy client. The money might not sound like much, but it adds up. Many editors use the work to support themselves while pursuing less remunerative careers in the arts or public service. "I'd be lying if I said that the pay didn't matter," says an editor who began working for EssayEdge while volunteering for Ameri-Corps. "I can make $25 to $40 an hour at this."

How Much Is Too Much?

The editors I interviewed for this story (most of whom requested anonymity) were divided on how far they were willing to go on an applicant's behalf. "Something important about EssayEdge is that we never write for the clients," says Katie Daily, who has had over 400 customers, some of whom have gotten into Columbia Business School, Harvard, and Brown. Another EssayEdge editor, though, sees things differently. He recalls one kid applying to MIT who wrote about a topic so inappropriate that the editor thought it was a joke. (Thanks to a nondisclosure agreement, the editor won't identify what the topic was, only that it was "the type of slap-happy thing that a bunch of guys hanging out at 2 in the morning would come up with.") But when the editor e-mailed the applicant, he "e-mailed back with the most sincere response imaginable about how he really was trying to write about this," the editor says. The finished essay was due in less than 48 hours, and the editor couldn't tell the kid to scrap the idea and start over. "The assumption on the part of the company was that the customers would be pissed if you did that," he says, adding that EssayEdge "keeps you in a state of low-level panic about losing your job." So he held his nose and dove in. "It was totally absurd, but I had to rewrite the essay. I used lots of scientific jargon—anything to make it a little less offensive. I was grasping at straws, any tendril of something that would make sense."

Other editors rationalize away ethical concerns by arguing that they're providing a public service. To them, essay editing is a form of affirmative action that levels the playing field for smart people who just happen to be bad writers, or for the foreign-born who don't write smoothly in English. "I firmly feel that my work, albeit in a limited way, is a source of stability and democratization," says the AmeriCorps volunteer/EssayEdge editor, with complete earnestness. "By helping future Asian tycoons come to America for their MBAs, I am helping strengthen the economic and personal ties between generations of leaders in America and Asia." Surprisingly, Harvey Mansfield, a Harvard professor famous for his condemnation of grade inflation, takes the position that this particular defense of essay editing might have merit. "I can see it in the case of foreigners," he says. "A lot of them have pretty good spoken English but don't write very well. And they

A flyer advertises the services of essay experts who assist prospective students with college admissions essays. Critics say the practice raises ethical concerns.

have to do all their work here in a foreign language, which is difficult for them. . . . That doesn't seem to be quite so serious."

Another Ethical Quandary

"The people that I was helping to get in were not traditional Ivy League people," adds a former editor for Admissions Essays, which sells custom-written "model" essays created from client questionnaire responses. "So I think that this is changing who gets in, but maybe for the better." (Admissions Essays posts a disclaimer saying that customers aren't allowed to use the essays the company generates as their own. But, the editor admits, "we all know that they do.")

Of course, the affirmative-action rationalization can cut both ways, particularly if you are a traditional—or at the very least stereotypical—Ivy League applicant. "There was one instance where it was the typical rich kid who didn't want to lift a finger," says the same former editor. He was applying to Harvard, Yale, and Brown, "and I could tell by reading the questionnaire that he was the kind of huge jerk that I had encountered too many times in college. He was a pompous asshole in the questionnaire, and I really wanted that pomposity to come though in the essay. I wanted the admissions committee to know what a jerk he was. So I did sort of adopt that tone in the essay. I don't think I was trying to make him not get in . . . well, maybe I was. I was thinking, We have quite enough of those people in the Ivy League."

The integrity of the edited essay can be even more compromised when the editors themselves are playing the admissions game, and stand to benefit from undermining the competition. Several years ago, another former editor for Admissions Essays wrote a few essays for clients who were seeking spots in the same law school that she was. When she got in, she was glad to discover that none of them had. "I don't know what I would've done at orientation weekend," she says, "if I had sat next to someone who I knew had cheated."

Cheating?

Cheated—it's a stinging accusation, but clients and their parents contend it doesn't apply. They feel they're not being any more dishonest than anyone else who secures some extra help. "I think it's no different from hiring a tutor," says one mother of a local public school student who used All Ivy Educational Services to polish his college essay. "My son put many hours into his essay and just needed help in editing it." A software company employee living in Bangalore who had the Writing Center edit his business school applications—and did not tell the schools that he'd used the service—adds, "An applicant's job is to make sure he communicated his ideas effectively. I see not much of a moral conflict in seeking professional help to edit your essays to ensure that your goals, motivation, hobbies, and career growth are all presented in a coherent manner. All the ideas expressed in the essays are completely mine."

Harvard professor Harry Lewis, former dean of Harvard College and author of Excellence Without a Soul, is unmoved. "Is it okay to impersonate people and take the SAT on their behalf?" he says. Justifications for using an editor, he feels, flow "from an assumption that it's better for a dishonest person who knows how to game the system to be admitted than an honest person who puts forward their own work and isn't as deceptive. . . . To say that what they're doing is completely fine, except that they don't want to reveal what they're doing? Horse manure."

Only One Factor

Admissions staff at Harvard, as well as at Amherst, Tufts, Boston University [BU], and UMass Amherst, declined to discuss how essay-editing services affect their decision-making process. But several schools said they don't think essay editing is corrupting the standards of elite education. "Remember, an essay is one component of a college application," says Colin Riley, a BU spokesman. "It is not a determining factor. So while it's important, no wonderfully written essay is going to alter the academic transcript or the recommendations from the teacher or the counselor or their standardized test scores."

MIT is the only top-tier school in town that's willing to condemn essay editing on the record. That's because recently an essay-editing company had the audacity to directly e-mail Ben Jones, an MIT admissions officer, asking for advice on what he was looking for. Bemused, Jones blogged his response on the MIT admissions website. "The rules are simple," he wrote. "Write your own essays."

"Having one's essay rewritten by someone else to the point that a reader wouldn't recognize the original is unethical, yes," he says, "but the more important issue is that applicants who engage in this sort of activity are really missing the point. At MIT, we're looking, quite simply, for the applicant's voice."

Implications

Amherst director of admissions Tom Parker says he's less concerned about individual essay scofflaws than about the broader implications of the trend. "What I worry about more is increasing the kind of cynicism that surrounds the whole process. Part of me wants to say, 'Let's just not admit anybody from any of these places where we know that students are doing this.' I've never done that and never will do that, but there are times when I really want to say, 'You know, we really don't need these kids.'"

At least for now, ferreting out the professionally tweaked imposters from the authentic essays isn't high on the to-do list of most admissions committees. But even if it were, essay editing has become such an unavoidable part of the application process, and such a vital source of employment for recent Ivy League grads, that it's probably here to stay. "It's like steroid use," says the editor for the Writing Center. "You can't compete unless you use it."

SEVEN

Women's Colleges Provide Advantages

Jessica Calefati

> According to Jessica Calefati's article, women's colleges are now very different places from the conservative atmosphere often depicted. At some women's colleges the majority of students are women of color, who see women's colleges as their best option for education and empowerment. Many women's colleges are now offering additional financial aid packages for women who might be economically disadvantaged, single mothers, or facing other challenges. Calefati says that women's colleges are, in many cases, more economically and ethnically diverse than their coeducational counterparts, and their graduates rate their educational experience more positively than do their peers.
>
> Calefati has written about education topics for *US News & World Report*, *Mother Jones*, and the *Newark (NJ) Star-Ledger*.

When it opens its admissions to men this fall [2009], Pennsylvania's Rosemont College will become the latest in a long line of former women's colleges to either go coeducational or shutter their doors. According to one study, just 3 percent of college bound women will even consider attending a women's college. Yet on many traditional coed campuses across the country, female students outnumber their male peers.

Some argue that this combination of factors demonstrates that women's colleges are obsolete, but Pat McGuire, who has served for 20 years as president of Trinity Washington University and its women's college, thinks otherwise. McGuire says she has watched Trinity (in the District of Columbia) transform during her tenure and looks no further than the admissions essays written by prospective students as a reminder of why women's colleges still exist and whom they are serving. "Where I come from," one applicant wrote, "based on stereotypes, the typical thing for me to do is become someone's 'baby mama' or housewife. Women all over are subjected to these stereotypes [and] that's why I firmly believe in this college."

Reaching a New Population

McGuire says that poor or minority women who see not just college but a women's college in particular as their ticket to knowledge, empowerment, and success are not the only students who appreciate what women's colleges have to offer. An analysis of data from the National Survey for Student Engagement shows women at women's colleges rate their educational experience higher than women at coeducational schools.

When more than 300 women's colleges existed in the early 1960s, these schools primarily served upper-middle-class, white students. The nearly 50 women's colleges still operating today are among the country's more ethnically and socioeconomically diverse liberal arts colleges, offering generous financial aid packages. Just as women's colleges originally were founded because women couldn't go to college elsewhere, many of today's women's colleges are surviving—and thriving—by educating specific populations of women who are still underserved.

Statistics

Though about 95 percent of Trinity's students were white when alumnae like House Speaker Nancy Pelosi and Kansas Gov.

Top Ten Women's Colleges

Barnard College, New York City, NY
Bryn Mawr College, Bryn Mawr, PA
Cedar Crest College, Allentown, PA
Mills College, San Francisco, CA
Mount Holyoke College, South Hadley, MA
Simmons College, Boston, MA
Smith College, Northampton, MA
Spelman College, Atlanta, GA
Sweet Briar College, Sweet Briar, VA
Wellesley College, Wellesley, MA

Taken from: Heidi Brown, "Why Women's Colleges Are Still Relevant," Forbes.com, August 12, 2009.

Kathleen Sebelius were students there, 85 percent of Trinity's current student body is either African-American or Hispanic. About half of the students hail from the D.C. metro area, and many women are the first in their family to go to college. Some are also the first in their families to graduate from high school, McGuire says. Although Trinity has little money for marketing and relies mostly on word of mouth to promote itself, the number of students enrolled in the university's women's college has risen by about 40 percent since 2000 to a record high of 600 students this spring semester. Trinity, like many of today's women's colleges, also enrolls part-time and professional students in coeducational programs to help financially support its historical women's college.

Because many of Trinity's women's college students arrive needing to improve their critical reading, writing, and math skills, the college recently rewrote its first-year curriculum to include a greater emphasis on developing these "foundational skills," McGuire says. "It's not that these women aren't smart or can't do it," she added. "It's that no one ever sat them down and explained how to do it." Like Trinity, Nebraska's College of St. Mary once had a primarily white student body. Today, about 20 percent of the student body at St. Mary's is made up of minority women, but what makes this Midwestern women's college stand out is the comprehensive support it provides for single mothers seeking a college education. Women in the Mothers Living and Learning [MLL] program live with their children alongside other single mothers in on-campus dorms, have access to free meals for their children in the college's dining hall, and can enroll their children in day-care services that are within walking distance of the college's campus.

Success Stories

Susan Williams lives in a St. Mary's dorm with two of her children and says the specialized program for single mothers attracted her to a women's college. Before transferring to St. Mary's, Williams attended the University of Missouri. At Mizzou, she lived in off-campus housing with her children but had little access to additional assistance. "At Mizzou, I was basically living on my own, and that didn't work for me. I needed more [emotional and academic] support," says Williams, who is studying to become an occupational therapist. "Women need women's colleges because for some women like me, it's the only way they will see where they can go in life."

When St. Mary's initiated its program for single mothers in 2000, just six mothers and their children were enrolled. Today, the program has grown to include 32 moms and their 38 children, who come from across the country to join the program. Sister Karen, a nun who runs the MLL program at St. Mary's, says she often finds mothers supporting other mothers in ways as simple as an hour of much-needed babysitting. "If one student's baby is out of control and Mom is frazzled, another mom is often there to knock on her door and say, 'Take a shower. I'll keep an eye on the baby while you take some time for you,'" Sister Karen says. "This level of support breeds success among these students, students who need to be successful not only for themselves but for their children, too."

Women's colleges, such as Virginia's Sweet Briar College (pictured), frequently offer financial packages for economically disadvantaged women.

Scholarship Packages

Virginia's Mary Baldwin College reaches specialized populations of women like the young, exceptionally gifted students who can attend the college as teenagers or women interested in joining an all-female corps of cadets, but the school also attracts women without the socioeconomic means to attend other colleges. Mary Baldwin President Pamela Fox says that 75 percent of her college's students receive need-based financial aid and that in response to the failing economy, Mary Baldwin students will have access to additional financial aid through the "Boldly Baldwin" program starting next fall.

The package offers 250 new first-year students a $2,000 merit award, an undetermined number of upperclassmen additional merit and need-based aid, and 50 students of all grade levels new on-campus internship positions where, she says, "we will put our own students to work." Fox says the Boldly Baldwin program is just one example of the many ways women's colleges turn to innovative ideas as a means to continue to attract new students. "Women's colleges are ahead of the curve and on the forefront of what women need," Fox says. "We have never been and we will never be followers. We have to create our own way forward."

EIGHT

Religious Students Can Succeed at Secular Colleges

Austin Webb

> Students who come to college with a strong religious background may have many questions about how to integrate their faith with their education, especially if they choose to attend a secular institution. In this viewpoint Austin Webb, a committed Christian who attended the California Institute of Technology (Caltech), separates fact from fiction for students and parents who are concerned about these issues. He assures readers that students with a mature foundation will be able to meet the challenges and pressures of college with confidence.
>
> Webb graduated with honors from Caltech in 2009 with a bachelor of science in theoretical computer science. He went on to graduate school at the University of Washington. With his mother and sister, he is part of Aiming Higher Consultants, a college admissions consulting business that serves the Christian and homeschooling communities.

There are lots of opportunities at [top colleges] . . . including first-rate instruction and unparalleled opportunities for internships, summer jobs, and research. In many cases, simply attending a particular institution gives instant credibility when it comes to applying for jobs or academic programs. Deserved or not, reputation is a powerful thing.

Almost as important is what one can gain from other students. Much of what I have learned at college so far, I learned from my peers. Every one of them are very academically talented and many of them arrived as freshmen already with near-expert knowledge of particular fields. Watching bright minds in action is an educational experience in itself.

However, there are many social benefits as well. A friend of mine at Caltech once remarked, "What makes this school so great is that absolutely everyone, down to the slacker who wastes most of his life in computer games, has a sparkle of life, a sense of humor, and a story to tell." College is one of the few times in life that exceptional students will be surrounded by peers who understand them and can challenge them intellectually.

Faith, Freedom, and Politics

Christians, though definitely a minority on most campuses, are far from scarce and in some cases appear to be on the rise, especially at science and engineering universities, according to my MIT contact. There is some hostility towards people of faith in modern higher education, but it is definitely not the rule. A friend from the University of Chicago, whom I will call Mary, recounted an experience from her freshman year: "I was in a philosophy class, working with several other students. One of them started saying ridiculous, hurtful things about Christianity. It did not last long, however. Several other students, none of whom were religious, took him to task and shut him down."

I can't speak for all campuses, but I've found the Christian community at Caltech to be far ahead of just about all other Christian groups of the same age range in terms of spiritual maturity. In fact, one young woman I know attends meetings of the Caltech Christian Fellowship instead of the equivalent group at her nearby Christian college. She said, "I tend to spend a lot of time with this group. They are more serious about their faith than people back at my school."

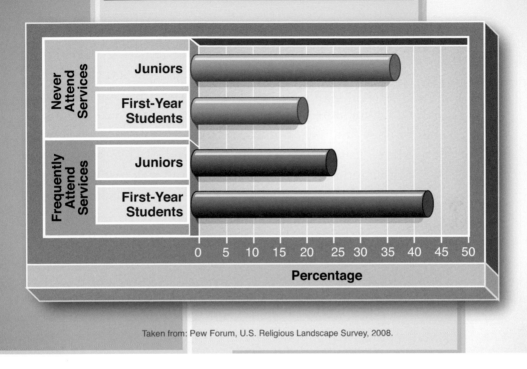

Percentage of Students Who Attend Religious Services

Taken from: Pew Forum, U.S. Religious Landscape Survey, 2008.

Christians and conservatives are no silent minority. At Harvard, one of the more notoriously liberal Ivies, the political left does not hold any monopoly on activism. My friend at Harvard, whom I will call Heather, said "It's definitely a marketplace. . . . The three most verbal, active campus groups seem to be the gay/lesbian association, the living wage/pro-immigration crowd, and the campus pro-life fellowship. I haven't seen any trace of a pro-abortion group. . . . The campus Democrats are definitely more numerous than the Republicans, but the Republicans are more energetic."

Problems That Probably Won't Be

Though it is important to keep the dangers of college in mind, don't spend time worrying about things that aren't general threats. Frankly, one of the most inaccurate and misleading stereotypes I've ever heard is that of the bullying, atheist professor ridiculing and corrupting good little Christian students in his class. Does it happen? Sure. But it is very, very rare. According to Mary, "The idea that academia is out to get Christians is a lie."

The vast majority of professors are fair and professional enough to not let their personal opinions, whatever those may be, bleed inappropriately into the classroom. The closest thing I got to a complaint was from Mary, who mentioned that one of her biology professors tended to be a bit sarcastic towards creationists. "But," she said, "he was kind of that way toward everyone, and always in a good humored way. Additionally, I was quite open about disagreeing with him in class and in some of my papers, and my grade didn't suffer for it."

There are real loonies out there, but I think you'll find that they tend to isolate themselves into fairly predictable areas, and are therefore easy to avoid. Generally, the wackiness occurs in less quantitative, academically lightweight disciplines like education, ethnic/gender studies, religious studies, and the like. Math, computer science, engineering, the hard sciences, and business tend to be apolitical or at least quite moderate. Government/political science, history, and literature vary a lot by school as to the degree of political correctness, so that has to be checked on a case-by-case basis. Basically, if you do your research and ask around about specific instructors before taking their classes, I doubt you'll have much trouble.

Parental Concerns

Christian parents, in my experience, tend to work overtime worrying about the amount of peer pressure their kids will be under in college. I can't speak for all cases, but seldom have I observed students to be pressured to do something against their beliefs. Mary observed that "If people know what your convictions are, like not drinking or practicing abstinence until marriage, they won't try to talk you into doing something contrary and will generally respect you for what you are."

Sending a student to college with their guard up about this kind of situation is kind of like building a tornado shelter in earthquake-prone California. Sure, it might be useful once in a great while, but you're taking a risk if focusing on imagined perils causes you to ignore real ones.

Matters of Real Concern

External circumstances can certainly influence behavior, but what I have found is that external pressures can only accomplish so much, for good or ill. People stand or fall based on what is within. The main danger to the Christian college student is losing their deliberateness and getting sloppy and inattentive when it comes to their relationships with Christ and with fellow Christians.

A student's first priority should be to spend time in prayer and scripture, and their next should be to plug into a solid Christian community on or near campus.

In my experience, this needs to happen quickly, or it won't happen at all. Research for this can start before departing for school.

Not just any Christian group will be suitable for the purpose. It needs to be a group that knows the student and that can keep him or her accountable. It needs to contain people more mature in the faith who have the time and inclination to act as mentors. For this reason, a local church can often be preferable to on-campus groups, which can sometimes be just glorified youth groups with questionable maturity. A friend of mine, who now works as a physicist, said, "If I had college to do over again, I would have invested more time in my local church than in the campus Christian group."

"No Such Thing as a Safe Place"

Some parents make the mistake of thinking that sending their children to a safe college environment will protect them. What they don't realize is that there is no such thing as a safe place.

Don't think that an institution with the label "Christian" on it is safe from those who would try to undermine a student's faith. Even without external prompting, what's inside will manifest eventually. I know of homeschoolers that went off to Christian colleges at which the "wrong crowd" was pretty hard to find . . . but they found it anyway. If a Christian college provides the education you need, by all means go to it. But never think of it as spiritual daycare for young adults.

Trouble won't usually come looking for your child, but it is always there if they are looking for it. Like an opportunistic infection, it generally only gets those who are weak and floundering to begin with. By ourselves we are not strong enough, but our Father is there to support and strengthen if we will only stay close to Him. Your prayers and continual communication (family cell phone plans can help a lot) with your student can help keep them centered and ensure that any adversity that comes along will only make them tougher.

Parents have to come to grips with the fact that they no longer have the ability to control the behavior of their offspring when they reach young adulthood. If they are not strong enough to resist the temptation and antagonism of a secular college, they probably won't be safe in a Christian college, either. Neither will they be safe in a job down the street from your home. It's time to fly, or to fall. If you've done your job, all that's left to do is pray for them.

Stuff to Put Up With

Perhaps more pervasive than things that might lead student astray are things that disrupt peace of mind. Drunkenness, obscenity, vulgarity, and the like are facts of life in higher education and a student will have to learn to ignore it and get on with life. However, most students are fairly reasonable, and "something that really, really outrages you, will probably outrage most of them also" according to Mary.

Choice of living quarters and roommates can be very important. On campuses where there is any freedom of choice in

The author recommends that a new college student take care to select a roommate having similar values and expectations.

housing, dorms generally get definite personalities, which can work either with or against the student. For instance, there is often at least one "party dorm" on each campus, where noise and other downsides of college life concentrate. Do your housing homework ahead of time—it can save you a lot of headaches.

Just as important are roommate issues. Most of the college horror stories I've heard are about "roommate incidents." If you have any choice in the matter of roommates, pick carefully and don't make the mistake of thinking that a good friend will necessarily make a good roommate. It was once remarked that "two people can be good friends, or roommates, but usually not both at the same time." If you are more introverted, as I am, you might benefit greatly from a private room, if one is available.

Parting Thoughts

Hopefully you now have a better idea what life at college is really like. There are problems, but I think you'll find that, if your student is mature (spiritually, intellectually, and emotionally) and remains centered, the experience will be overwhelmingly rewarding.

For me, the issue is much bigger than my personal benefit and experience. I chose a top-tier institution because the academy is probably the most important marketplace of ideas on earth. It is the place where movers and shakers are made. It is important that the Christian faith and life be on display with all the other philosophies of our age, so that others may see the truth in it.

NINE

Church-Sponsored Colleges Do Not Always Promote Religious Values

Ian Hunter

> Churchgoing teens who hope to continue their spiritual experiences in college might be drawn to church-sponsored colleges or universities. But as Ian Hunter writes here, not all church-sponsored schools are created equal. He provides an example of one university that seems to be distancing itself from its Christian origins and one college whose actions often seem at odds with its Catholic label. The author advises students and parents to do their research and not to take religious labels for granted.
>
> Hunter is professor emeritus in the faculty of law at the University of Western Ontario.

Parents of students who are completing high school sometimes spend anxious hours scrutinizing college and university calendars in search of a Christian higher education for their son or daughter. Herewith, a cautionary tale.

Valparaiso University was founded by Methodists in 1859. It shut down briefly (1871–3) during the American Civil War, then re-opened as a Methodist College (although called a "Normal School"). In 1925 it became a Lutheran University, initially run by clergy, and dedicated to the glory of God in the Lutheran tradition. Even today its 'mission statement' makes reference to " . . . the Lutheran tradition of scholarship, freedom and faith."

Over the decades of the 20th century, Valparaiso University, like many other Christian colleges and universities, has gradually relinquished its Christian identity. Valparaiso University's website boasts that since 2008 it is a "tobacco-free" campus; not just the weed, but also the seed, has been left behind.

Political Correctness

A report from a Valparaiso "Task Force" (Odd, isn't it, how that militaristic term escapes censure even in the politically-correct hothouse of the modern University?) recommended changes to the University Convocation: out with the Valparaiso hymn, in with the "Alma Mater Song" to make " . . . the Valparaiso University spirit . . . more inclusive for the increasingly diverse student body." In fact, to insure "hospitality" and "welcome," hymns should

"Forget it, Sister Jessica — Notre Dame doesn't *need* cheerleaders."

"Forget it, Sister Jessica, Notre Dame doesn't need Cheerleaders" Cartoon by Baloo-Rex May/www.CartoonStock.com © Baloo-Rex May. Reproduction rights obtainable from www.CartoonStock.com.

be dropped altogether at public events. Convocation should also avoid Scripture readings, substituting instead " . . . readings in keeping with the spirit of the Convocation or in harmony with academic or campus wide themes." Care is required to " . . . avoid the kind of overt religiosity that can be misperceived as exclusionary." Ah yes, one might just about recall the kind of "overt and exclusionary religiosity" that once led someone a long time ago to declare: "No one comes to the Father but by me."

Once such vestiges of parochialism have been purged, the Task Force assures the reader that Valparaiso will " . . . continue to robustly celebrate its rich Lutheran/Christian tradition while remaining sensitive to the feelings of those who belong to different faith communities."

Still a Religious School?

Never mind that different faith communities have countless secular universities to attend. No, henceforth Valparaiso will direct its recruitment to groups under-represented in American higher education. And who, pray tell (if such a colloquialism is permissible) might they be? Why, " . . . people of different sexual orientation and gender identities."

So, there you have it. By such means do denominational colleges and universities sever their ties to the Christian faith that gave them birth, the faith that nourished them and enabled them to flourish. Now the dogma of the Christian faith is seen as judgmental, non-inclusive, and reactionary. The once-Christian university wants instead to hitch its wagon to the new religion called secular postmodernism. The plain truth is that universities like Valparaiso are embarrassed by their Christian origins; they are inimical to Christian doctrine; they want to be secular institutions. So why not just come out and say so? Simple, because to say so might give offence to their "donor base."

Secular Education with a Christian Label

So that is the story of Valparaiso University, but it is also the story of Canadian colleges and universities.

Opposed to President Barack Obama's pro-choice position, students at the Catholic University of Notre Dame hold an alternate graduation ceremony on May 17, 2009, to protest his address at the school's commencement ceremony.

Take the example with which I am most familiar—King's University College, a Catholic college at the University of Western Ontario [UWO]. A student enrolling at King's will receive the same postmodern course of studies as he or she would receive on the main UWO campus. His or her degree will come from Western, not Kings. Pretty much the only difference is that some courses will be taken within sight of a crucifix on the wall.

In other words, the King's student will receive a secularized education under an ostensibly Catholic roof. But when being

Catholic might actually mean something—as, for example, when UWO decided to award an honourary degree to Canada's most notorious abortionist, Henry Morgentaler—being a King's student made not the slightest difference. Indeed, the then-principal of King's was a member of the Senate Honourary Degrees Committee that decided to bestow the honour on Morgentaler.

So parents of university age students, who are considering where to send their children for what passes for "higher education," should not be deluded by a Christian or Catholic label. Look behind the facade and you may well discover a postmodern institution indifferent, or worse, hostile, to the precepts of the Christian faith.

TEN

Student Athletes Consider Many Factors When Choosing a College

Jim Gerweck

Competitive athletes have special factors to keep in mind as they consider their college choices. In many cases, these high-achieving athletes are being actively recruited by major universities, which can provide additional pressures during an already busy and stressful time. In this viewpoint Jim Gerweck provides brief glimpses into the decision-making process undergone by three college runners. Two of the three runners wound up choosing colleges close to their hometowns; one went across the country. For all three, the reputation of the school's athletic programs—and their coaches' reputations in particular—were especially important.

Gerweck is managing editor for *Running Times* magazine. In addition, Gerweck is involved with the committee of USA Track & Field that certifies distances for road racing courses.

The college admission process is a harrowing one for most high school seniors, with the pressure of SATs and transcripts, essays and applications making it one of the most trying times of anyone's life. It's much the same for the top scholastic runners in the country, although for somewhat different reasons.

Unlike the majority of their peers, athletic blue-chippers don't have to worry as much about being accepted as they do about picking from dozens, perhaps hundreds, of schools that are recruiting them. In a turnabout from the normal high school senior's experience, the main concern is choosing rather than being chosen. It might seem like a pleasant problem to have, but it doesn't make life any less stressful, as recruiting letters and phone calls and official campus visits add to an already busy schedule.

Three of the top runners from the class of 2009—Jordan Hasay, Kathy Kroeger and Trevor Dunbar—reveal some of the thought process that went into their final decisions.

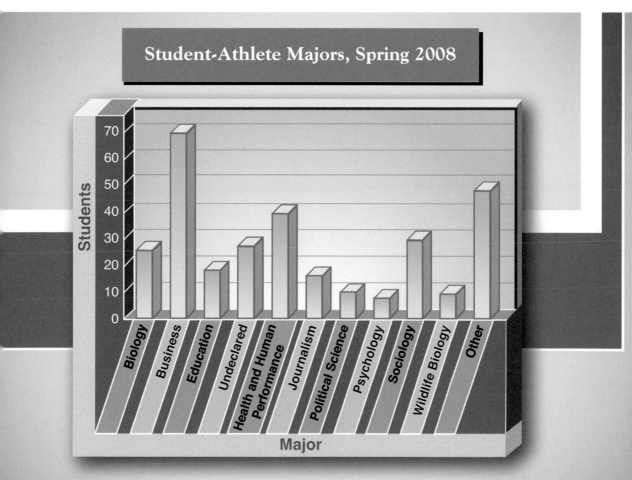

Taken from: University of Montana, 2008.

Do Your Research

Jordan was one of the most decorated runners to come through the American high school ranks in the past decade, sandwiching Foot Locker national championships as a freshman and a senior around medals in the world junior track meet and a finalist spot in the U.S. Olympic trials 1500m, where she set a high school record of 4:14.50. She was the last of the three to announce her college decision, waiting until the day before the national signing period on Feb. 4 to make her somewhat surprising decision to go to the University of Oregon.

"You have to go where you feel it's right for you," she said prior to making her choice public. "Try to picture yourself at that school. You have to make sure you're confident in your decision." Jordan was 90 percent sure after visiting Oregon in the fall, but wanted to make certain she'd explored all her options. "I almost cancelled my last two visits, but I wanted to be sure I'd seen all the schools." Jordan advises potential recruits to do a lot of research ahead of time and narrow their choices down to a manageable number.

The Right Fit

Kathy, who succeeded Jordan as Foot Locker champ in 2006, began looking at schools her junior year. "I knew I was looking for someplace with good academics, particularly in science and math," she says. During her junior year spring break, she visited several schools unofficially. Once the recruiting process began in earnest, she narrowed her choices to Wisconsin, Stanford and Duke. "When I came back from visiting them, I knew it was going to be a hard choice," she recalls. "All the coaches were great." After talking to her coach, Olympian Jim Spivey, she sat down and analyzed all her choices. "Ultimately, at Stanford I felt like I really belonged. That, and their history of producing so many Olympians, decided me." Also, the move to the West Coast was a factor. Kathy wanted college to be "really different" from high school in Tennessee. She made her choice on New Year's Eve and says, "I was so relieved—I couldn't stop smiling."

Although superior high school athletes are frequently recruited by colleges, a number of them consider all facets of a school and not merely its athletic program in deciding which to attend.

Great Coaching

Trevor couldn't do much smiling at that time—he'd just had four wisdom teeth removed—but he was equally happy and relieved to have finalized his college choice as well.

Coming from Kodiak, Alaska, Trevor's college environment would almost have to be different, but he chose to stay relatively close to home by attending the University of Portland.

"Every coach I met had knowledge to offer me and improve my running, but Portland kind of won out because I felt the most comfortable there," he says. "What set it apart was the area, the small environment of the school, running trails and surroundings—it was a place I could enjoy for the next four years." There was also a personal connection to UP—his parents met there, and his mother was a top runner for the Pilots.

Another big factor was coach Rob Conner's track record of taking good high school runners and developing them, through a program of long distance mileage, into some of the top collegians in the country, able to hold their own against more decorated recruits from other schools. As the Foot Locker runner-up, Trevor is doubtless the best high schooler to matriculate to Portland. "I'm hoping I get the same effect that everyone else has there," he says.

ELEVEN

Students on the Autism Spectrum Should Determine Whether College Is Right for Them

Ernst VanBergeijk

In this viewpoint Ernst VanBergeijk gives students who are on the autism spectrum, as well as their parents and caregivers, important questions to consider as they decide which college to choose—or whether a traditional college is the right choice at all. The questions can be addressed to administrators and guidance counselors at traditional degree programs as well as vocational schools and programs specifically designed to teach independent living skills to students with special needs. The author also strongly suggests visiting any programs under consideration prior to making any decision.

VanBergeijk is the executive director of New York Institute of Technology's Vocational Independence Program, which enables students with significant learning disabilities to maximize their potential for independence. He is also a research associate in the autism unit of the Yale Child Study Center's Developmental Disabilities Clinic. He has more than twenty years' experience as a social worker and psychologist.

Deciding what to do after high school is a daunting task for any young person, but for students on the autism spectrum, the thought can be paralyzing. Additional questions need to be asked and answered to insure a goodness of fit between the student's strengths, goals, and weaknesses and a post secondary educational program's strengths, goals, and weaknesses. Below are 10 questions students on the autism spectrum need to ask program administrators before deciding to enroll in a college degree, vocational or independent living skills program.

1. What does a student receive when he or she completes the program?

Graduates will receive either a degree or a certificate of completion. Degree programs allow students to apply for federally guaranteed student loans and grants. Students in these programs must complete Free Application for Federal Student Aid (FAFSA) applications. Students in certificate programs, on the other hand, must apply for continuing education loans through a private bank or lender.

2. Is the program accredited and by whom?

Reputable college programs are accredited by the Middle States Commission on Higher Education. Do not attend a Bachelor's degree program that has not been accredited by Middle States Commission. The degree will not be recognized as legitimate. Vocational and Independent Living Programs may be accredited by other agencies such as state offices of vocational rehabilitative services or other social service entities.

3. How is the program funded?

This simple question will also give you an idea of the agencies that give the program legitimacy. Degree programs that have students using FAFSA loans are endorsed, at least implicitly, by the federal government. State offices of developmental disability services or vocational rehabilitative services may pay for some vocational and independent living programs. Local school districts may also fund students' attendance in these latter two types of programs through Individualized Education Program (I.E.P.) Transition Plans.

Percentage of College Students with a Disability

Incoming first-year students reporting a disability/medical condition, by sex (percentages):

Disability/Medical Condition	Men	Women	All Students
Attention-deficit/hyperactivity disorder (ADHD)	6.4	3.8	5.0
Psychological disorder (depression, etc.)	2.6	4.9	3.8
Learning disability (dyslexia, etc.)	3.1	2.7	2.9
Physical disability (speech, sight, mobility, hearing, etc.)	2.7	2.7	2.7
Chronic illness (cancer, diabetes, autoimmune disorders, etc.)	1.3	2.1	1.8
Other	2.8	3.6	3.3
One reported disability/medical condition	11.9	11.9	11.9
Two or more reported disabilities/medical conditions	2.5	2.9	2.7

Taken from: Higher Education Research Institute, "The American Freshman: National Norms Fall 2010," Research Brief, January 2011.

4. What are the credentials of the program's administrative, teaching and service delivery staff?

Ideally, these professionals should have the highest degrees and licenses possible in their respective fields and in the area of autism spectrum disorders [ASDs].

5. What special training, if any, does the program staff receive on ASDs?

Not only should the staff have training in intervention techniques with this population, but also other information that is important in educating these students. This information should include co-morbid psychiatric disorders, medications and their effects, and the diversity of this population. Since many of these students have other medical issues, training in CPR [cardiopulmonary resuscitation], first aid, and the use of automatic external defibrillator devices is warranted.

6. *What are the staffing ratios?*

In a college program the faculty to student ratio can be as high as 1:600 in introductory classes held in large lecture halls. College Disabled Student Services Offices frequently have caseloads of

At West Virginia's Marshall University Autism Training Center, a college senior works with an autistic student. Some universities offer degree programs that teach independent living skills to students with special needs.

one counselor to 350 learning-disabled students. Vocational and independent living skills programs will generally have much lower ratios.

7. How much flexibility is inherent in the program?

Students in post secondary education often change their minds regarding college majors, which ultimately affects their career trajectory. However, some students on the spectrum may learn that they either do not have the skills or interest in completing a liberal arts education. Rather, they would prefer to pursue a vocation such as computer programming or repair. Does the program have the flexibility for the students to transfer from an academic track to a vocational track or vice-versa?

8. Does the post secondary program offer any summer preview programs for high school students?

Summer programs are an excellent way to judge the goodness of fit between the student and the academic year program. It also helps the student learn what the social environment will be in the fall, allows them to forge new friendships, and demystifies the notion of going away to school. Summer programs allow the student to become comfortable with the environment and the routine, before the academic pressures of the fall semester begin. Consequently, summer programs may act as stress inoculators, helping prevent student drop out.

9. What information can a parent expect from the program regarding the academic progress and behavior of his or her son or daughter?

The students are presumably 18-year-old adults when they enter a post secondary program. Under the Family Education Privacy Act of 1974 (FERPA), students over the age of 18 have the right to privacy. The law prevents third parties from gaining access to a student's educational records without his or her written consent. When the student reaches 18 years old, his or her parents become a third party. Find out how the college or program deals with this situation. Often the program will have the student sign a release of information if necessary, so the program can speak to the parents.

10. What is the program's philosophy and how do they handle interpersonal conflict among the students?

Many students on the spectrum will have interpersonal conflicts. Parents may expect programs to act quite proactively and to take into account the student's social disability. The parents may want to get involved in the resolution of the conflict. Often this is not appropriate. Programs will have a philosophy that teaching social skills is a part of the educational process and view the conflict as a learning opportunity or view the conflict as a disciplinary matter. Ask questions to get a sense of how they handle conflicts involving students on the spectrum.

Other Considerations

Asking questions of the administrative staff is only one part of the decision making process. Visit the programs while school is in session. See the programs in action and ask the students their experiences with the program. Ask them their likes and dislikes about the program. Finally, the prospective student needs to ask him or herself, "Can I picture myself here with these students?" If the answer is yes, then this program may be a good fit.

TWELVE

Rejection Is Not the End of the World

Scott Dobson-Mitchell

> When he was applying for colleges, Canadian student Scott Dobson-Mitchell had his heart set on a specific program at McMaster University in Hamilton, Ontario. It seemed to have everything he would need for a satisfying undergraduate experience and would also give him the best possible training for his post-collegiate goals. But Dobson-Mitchell was not accepted by that particular program, although he was accepted at a number of other fine schools, including a different program at McMaster. In this article he writes about the disappointment of rejection but also about the surprising discovery that, as he writes, "Sometimes Plan B turns out better than Plan A."
>
> Dobson-Mitchell started his writing career at age twelve, writing a column for his local paper until he graduated from high school. He is now a student at University of Waterloo in Waterloo, Ontario. Dobson-Mitchell also writes and cartoons about college admissions and university life for the *Maclean's* On Campus website.

Microscopes. Lab coats. Dead bodies. What's not to love? Yes, I'm talking about the perfect pre-med program—in this case, health sciences at McMaster University.

In my last year of high school, when filling out university applications, health sciences at McMaster seemed like a perfect fit. I knew that after my undergraduate degree, I wanted to study medicine, and McMaster's program has all the prerequisites built in. It gives students lab experience, and it's focused on biology, my favourite subject area.

The Top Choice

The more I read about the program, the more I wanted in. Health sciences at McMaster was my first-choice program. But I knew the odds. A minimum 90 per cent average is required for consideration, but in order to be competitive you need to be in the low 90s at the very least.

Med schools across Canada claim they'll consider any undergraduate degrees—meaning, it doesn't matter if you have a degree in biology, anthropology, engineering or drama. It's your GPA that really counts. Most med schools still have prerequisite courses, like organic chemistry, microbiology and physics. You can apply to med school with a music degree, but you still need to have all of those mandatory courses. The beauty of McMaster's health sciences: after completing the program, you have all the necessary prerequisites to apply to any med school across Canada.

Oh, there's also the fact that Mac students get to experiment with cadavers. Seriously.

Tough Questions

A 90+ average isn't the only thing you need to get in. There's also the mandatory supplementary application—essays and personal questions, including a few, well, odd ones. One asks, "What's one extracurricular activity that's important to your sense of self and why?" There's only one thing worse than a meandering, open-ended, self-exploration kind of question like that. And that's question No. 2: "What is the one question that shouldn't be asked and why?" (I knew instinctively not to write,

Admission Rates of Selected Colleges and Universities, 2011

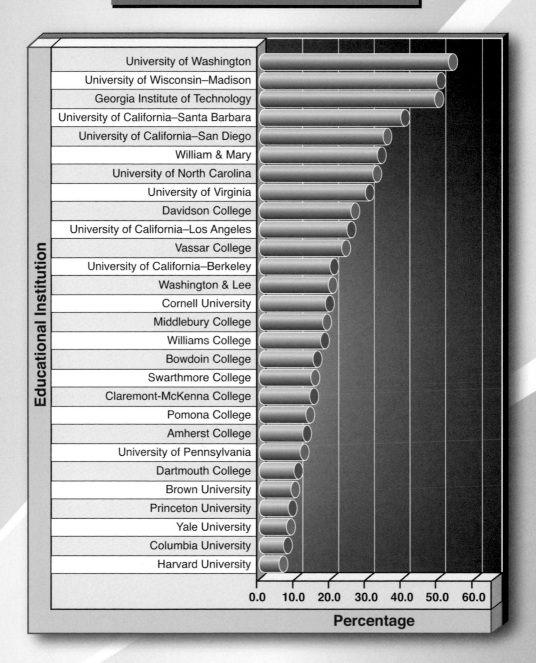

"Have you accepted Jesus Christ as your personal Lord and Saviour?")

Unlike with real estate, when it comes to choosing a university, location isn't the most important criteria. Sure, it matters. But when I decided health sciences at McMaster was my first-choice program, it wasn't because it had the most convenient location. After all, I live within 15 minutes of the University of Waterloo and Wilfrid Laurier. But health sciences at McMaster was still number one. It was meant to be.

A Big Disappointment

Fast forward several months. Early acceptances were being mailed out. And finally, it arrived: the letter from McMaster.

I almost didn't want to open it. My entire future was riding on this letter. If I got into the program, I was one step closer to med school. Had my marks been competitive enough? Did my essay convey my sense of self well enough?

I opened the letter: "After careful consideration, we are not able to offer you admission at this time."

I didn't get in. I had been rejected. I read the letter again and again, hoping to see something like, "Nah, we're just messing with you. You've been accepted!"

I had offers from the biology programs at McMaster, Waterloo and Toronto, along with health studies and honours biomedical sciences at Waterloo. But who wants the consolation prize? I hadn't gotten into my first-choice program.

What now?

Plan B

Well, sometimes, Plan B turns out better than Plan A. In the end, accepting the offer for the honours biomedical sciences program at Waterloo wasn't a compromise. Sure, I don't get to experiment with cadavers. But as the University of Waterloo's website states, "Waterloo's highly flexible biomedical sciences program can prepare you for almost any health profession program in North America." Oh, and as the website also points out,

Based on his own experience, the author cautions prospective college students that a rejection letter from a highly desired college does not mean that other colleges cannot meet the student's expectations.

all the prerequisite courses for almost every med school in North America are built right into the program.

Biomedical sciences at Waterloo also allows students lots of electives, so they can customize the program to meet their individual preferences. You have the freedom to take a variety of courses, enabling you to pursue that interest in photography, medieval literature or abstract art. Not to mention that a well-balanced schedule can be a lifesaver when you're weighed down with physics, organic chemistry and cell biology courses.

I'm now in my second year of the program at Waterloo. I still remember how I felt after sending out my applications—like my entire life was hanging in the balance, completely dependent on getting into my first-choice program. If I could have pushed an instant beam-into-McMaster's-health-sciences-program button, I would have. But then I wouldn't have ended up where I am today, truly enjoying my courses and labs, and actually looking forward to microbiology lectures.

Maybe I would have enjoyed McMaster's health sciences program just as much. Or maybe I wouldn't have. Either way, I didn't get into my first-choice program. And it wasn't the end of the world.

THIRTEEN

The Ivy League Is Not the Best Choice for Every High-Achieving Student

Peter Vartanian

As a high-achieving high school student, Peter Vartanian came to the same conclusion as thousands of other students like himself—the schools of the Ivy League were his best academic option for college. In Vartanian's case, he was particularly interested in Brown University. When he was rejected by Brown, however, Vartanian realized that there are certainly advantages to academically solid but lower-profile schools like the one he ultimately chose. These include a welcoming atmosphere and a chance to be a standout student rather than just one of countless overachievers, not to mention generous financial aid and scholarship packages for top students like Vartanian. Once he broadened his scope beyond the Ivies, Vartanian found the school that was perfect for him after all.

Vartanian is a student at Creighton University in Omaha, Nebraska, where he studies communication and graphic design.

Reaching is great, but be careful not to overlook a less-well-known winner. The more pragmatic choice might just turn out to be your ideal one, too.

In the summer of 2008, after my junior year at Dominican High School outside Milwaukee, I would say "Olly olly oxen free" every time I heard the ominous word "college," hoping somehow to keep the end of childhood at bay. The application process loomed, and I saw it as daunting. Rather than prepare for SATs or college essays, I was wondering what happened to my kindergarten vow to attend a school a few miles from home so I could eat lunch with my mom. Farewell, sweet naïveté.

Soon enough, I had to play the admissions game. After browsing for hints and how-tos on the Internet, I was less intimidated by the prospect. And, having decided to study graphic design, I even had a hunch that a portfolio of my artwork might be in order. However, I struggled with the decision about where to apply. Should I be pragmatic, or try for what I thought would be the ideal school—regardless of how realistic (or unrealistic) that goal might be?

Ivy League Blinders

I opted to "reach," convinced that my dream school was an elite private institution with a relatively small student body. I came up with seven schools, and Brown University topped my list. I confess that some of the reasons for this choice were strictly clichés. To me, Brown seemed to gleam with prestige. At the same time, its superb academics and flexible curriculum would provide an optimal environment where I could cultivate my talents.

The $50,560-per-year price tag did prompt an interesting talk with my parents about financial realities. But we put aside our differences, and afterward I agreed to remain open to other options. One of those was Creighton University, which I regarded (albeit reluctantly) as a potential winner. I had enjoyed my visit to the Omaha school during the summer and had felt comfortable there. Creighton even offered a graphic-design major. In hindsight, it was only my urgent need to attach myself

to an Ivy League school that kept me from giving Creighton more serious consideration as a possible first choice.

Switching Gears

I seized on Brown's motto, "In God we hope"—and I did. But come April, it turned out that all my fervor and hope in God weren't enough to gain me admission. Brown turned me down. I was disappointed, maybe even a little disillusioned. But those feelings passed quickly. I realized I was the same person as before —that rejection hadn't stripped me of my capabilities or confidence. I still believed I could succeed at Brown but realized that I likely wouldn't have been a standout there. But the same passions that I'd hoped would win over Brown might enable me to emerge from the student pack as a leader elsewhere. I pinned the rejection letter on my bedroom wall, and I actually smiled.

Admittedly, the smile came easier because I had another option. A few months earlier I had been accepted to Creighton. When I was still under the sway of Brown, my admission to Creighton felt like a consolation prize. But as I thought more about the school, I realized it just might be the right place for me. It not only fit all my original criteria but had also radiated such warm, hospitable vibes during my visit that I'd felt as if I were only a few miles from home. With a proud tradition bolstered by generous scholarship opportunities, Creighton now

*Initially rejected by a leading Ivy League school, Brown
University, the author chose Creighton University (pictured),
a solid, low-profile school that exceeded his expectations.*

appeared to me in a different light—as both an ideal and a pragmatic choice.

In my high school's production of *The Wiz*, I played the titular con artist from Omaha, whose misadventure with a hot-air balloon lands him in Oz. The Wiz believes, above all, in the benefits of "power, prestige, and money." But of course the Wiz is a fraud. So on campus in Omaha, I will try to keep those aspirations in their rightful place. Perhaps on my way to school I will stop to admire a cornfield, or even spot a balloon among some cumulus fluff. Maybe I didn't have to bid goodbye to sweet naïveté after all.

FOURTEEN

Community Colleges Are the Right Option for Many Students

Mark Rowh

In this article Mark Rowh, a long-time advocate for and expert in community college education offers readers seven reasons to seriously consider community college as they weigh their college options. These include practical considerations such as price, convenience, and career preparation as well as more intangible qualities such as community colleges' ability to ease the transition between high school and college and the teaching quality of their faculty. Whether students transfer from a community college to a four-year school or conclude their education with an associate's degree, Rowh says, these are valuable considerations to take into account.

Rowh, a vice president at New River Community College in Virginia, is an experienced community college educator and author of twenty books and five hundred magazine articles. His articles have appeared in *Reader's Digest, Consumers Digest, Career World, American Careers, Careers & Colleges, Minority Engineer,* and *Private Colleges and Universities.* His books include *Coping with Stress in College* and the *Community College Companion.*

Have you thought about attending a community college? Whether for full-time studies or simply earning credits to be used later at another school, a two-year college can be a smart choice.

Some students never consider community college. They know that two-year schools lack the status of big-name universities and elite private colleges. But for a variety of reasons, more students are giving them a try. Nearly half the college students in the United States are enrolled in community, junior, or technical colleges. "Community colleges are becoming more popular," says Rebecca Craft, college relations director at Delaware Technical and Community College. "They are convenient, cost-efficient, and flexible."

How do you know if a community college would work for you? Here are seven reasons why attending a two-year college can pay off.

Big Money Saver

Community colleges are less expensive than four-year colleges.

"Two-year colleges give you the same education at a much cheaper price," says Monique Serrell, a student at Mount Hood Community College in Oregon. "I am able to attend a two-year college at half the cost that I would pay at a four-year school."

A year's tuition and fees average less than $2,100 at two-year colleges, according to the American Association of Community Colleges (AACC). That's much less than four-year schools, with most public colleges costing three to five times that amount and many private colleges charging $20,000 to $30,000 or more per year.

Moreover, a worker with a two-year associate's degree earns an average of $6,000 more per year than a worker with only a high school diploma, according to the U.S. Department of Labor.

At the same time, a student who wants to go on and earn a four-year degree may enjoy the best of both worlds. "If you go two years to a community college and then transfer to a four-year school, you can get the benefit of a degree from a name school at half the cost," says Anson Smith, public relations co-ordinator for Housatonic Community College in Bridgeport, Conn. If you choose to work while completing your degree, some employers will even help pay for education costs.

Many community colleges have developed arrangements with four-year schools to make it easier for students to transfer. For example, the Community College of Denver offers a "campus pipeline" program in which its courses are specially aligned to be accepted at partner institutions.

Close to Home
Community colleges are convenient.

As the name implies, community colleges exist to serve their local communities. No matter where you live, chances are a community college lies within driving distance: Nearly 1,200 public and private two-year colleges are in operation today.

If you don't want to go away to school, or if that's not possible, attending a local community college can be a convenient option.

"Community colleges are close by, so you don't have to pay to live in a dorm," says Mark Schaefer, a student at New York's Dutchess Community College. "You already know where everything is around you, and if you have a job, you don't have to quit or take time off." Schaefer drives about 15 minutes to reach his campus, where he holds a part-time job during the week.

Confidence Booster
Community colleges help ease the transition between high school and higher education.

When Kally Davis graduated from her Arizona high school, she didn't feel ready to take on a big university. So she enrolled at Mesa Community College in Phoenix. There, Davis thrived on the personal attention offered by instructors, staff, and other students. She did well academically, and her confidence grew. After graduating, she enrolled at Arizona State University.

"I was able to achieve so much academically and socially because of the smaller environment," she says of her community college experience. "I was able to get to know more of my classmates, and having a smaller class size also made the instructors more accessible to the students. It was wonderful to get to know my teachers on a personal basis."

Of course, not all four-year colleges are big, and many small, private colleges offer a high level of personal attention. But for the combination of individual attention and low cost, a community college can be ideal for many students.

Caitlin O'Rourke, a student at Albuquerque Technical Vocational Institute in New Mexico, agrees. "For a high school student considering a four-year degree of any kind, the smartest place to begin is a community college," she says. "It is a much kinder, gentler place to get one's feet wet in the world of academia."

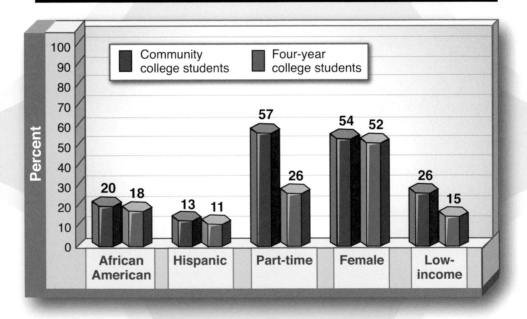

Florida's Community Colleges Attract a Different Demographic than Do Its Four-Year Colleges

Taken from: Diane Furchtgott-Roth, Louis Jacobsen, and Christie Mokher, *Strengthening Community Colleges' Influence on Economic Mobility*, 2009, Economic Mobility Project, an Iniative of the Pew Charitable Trusts.

Great Teaching

Community colleges employ dynamic teachers.

Holly Lowman thought her instructors at the two-year College of Southern Maryland were excellent. When she went on to Bowie State University, Lowman was pleased to find that her community college professors compared favorably with those at the university. "I feel that the quality of teaching was equal to or better than the four-year institution," she says.

Perhaps the best-kept secret about community colleges is the strength of the faculty. Most professors at two-year colleges see themselves as teachers rather than researchers. They focus their energy on helping students succeed. "Our faculty [members] love to teach and have chosen to dedicate themselves to the classroom rather than to focus their energy on research interests," says Barbara Risser, vice president of student and academic services at the State University of New York at Onondaga Community College. "Students at community colleges will not be taught by graduate students."

Thanks to the quality of teaching in two-year colleges, students who transfer to universities are generally well prepared to succeed at the next level. "I had many professors who pushed me to become a better learner," Lowman says.

Honors Courses

Honors programs appeal to talented students.

Are you a superstar in science, the arts, or some other area? Many community colleges offer honors programs, which help good students stay motivated and can provide a pipeline to four-year schools.

For example, New York's Rockland Community College offers an honors program in business, accounting, computer studies, and entrepreneurship. Students complete internships and many go on to top-tier schools, such as the Wharton School of Business of the University of Pennsylvania and the Stern School of Business at New York University. "My honors course was the most rewarding and challenging course I've ever taken," says Katie Edgerton, a student at Monroe Community College in New York. "I feel better prepared for my future at a four-year university."

Students at community colleges around the country are eligible for membership in Phi Theta Kappa (PTK), the national honor society for community colleges. More than 600 colleges and universities offer scholarships for PTK members.

Hot Jobs
Career programs offer fast tracks to good jobs.

Are you eager to get right into the workforce? Community colleges offer a wide array of programs that can be completed in one or two years. Hot career program areas in two-year schools include biotechnology, geographic information systems (GIS), computer network administration, Web site design, medical imaging, nursing, and paralegal studies, to name just a few. "Community colleges provide market-driven education," Smith says. "They're in tune with the education and training needs of businesses in surrounding areas, and they respond to them."

Outstanding Support
Support services are wide-ranging.

When Donna Baust began her studies at the Community College of Baltimore County in Maryland, she was impressed by the range of support provided to students. "Tutoring is free, and there are computers and printers located all over campus for the students who would not otherwise have access to them," Baust says.

Need help with computers? Want to improve your writing ability? Don't have a clue about what career to pursue? You'll find programs and services available to help, generally for no additional cost.

"The Support services at community colleges are wonderful," says Kim Poast, dean of students at the Community College of Denver. "These services are open to any student who wants them, and they range from tutoring assistance and help

Community colleges, such as New Jersey's Raritan Valley Community College (pictured), are known for providing superior support services for their students.

with financial issues to academic planning or assistance with getting involved on campus."

Along with academic support, two-year schools often offer special services, such as note takers for students with learning disabilities and interpreters for hearing-impaired students.

Candice Hernandez has epilepsy. A student at Seminole Community College in Florida, she needs to keep a seizure-alert dog with her while attending classes. Hernandez says that security officers, instructors, and other staff accommodate her dog and are quick to help out if she suffers a seizure.

"They're absolutely great when it comes to dealing with people with disabilities," Hernandez reports. "Whenever I've gotten sick, I've never had to worry about the staff or the security. I don't feel that if I was attending a big four-year college that I would be able to rely on anyone to help me [the way] I can at my community college."

Community college can offer a solid bridge between high school and a career; it may be worth considering for all or part of your own journey.

FIFTEEN

Students Should Consider Taking a Year Off Between High School and College

Tim Engle

The concept of taking a "gap year" (a year off) between high school and college has been an accepted option in the United Kingdom and Europe for many years but has only recently gained notice in the United States. However, as Tim Engle points out in this viewpoint, options abound for US students who wish to take some time off before entering a college or university. Some students use the time to pursue an individual passion in a concentrated way. Others, the author says, choose to participate in volunteer service projects or to spend a year working and saving money, while some travel. As this viewpoint reveals, students who are mature enough to handle this unstructured time often come out of it with renewed energy and excitement once they do begin their college careers.

Engle is a writer/editor for the *Kansas City Star*.

The so-called gap year between high school and college is just what some students need.

Grant Stauffer is willing to admit it. He slacked off his first couple of years of high school. He eventually got on track, but "my parents still believe there's a little more maturing I need to do, especially as far as my whole work ethic goes."

So Stauffer, 18, a newly minted high school graduate, will not be heading to college this fall. Instead, he's taking a "gap year," delaying frat parties and the rest of the college experience by one year.

A Micro Trend

The gap year option seems to be picking up steam—Stauffer's high school paper, reporting plans of the Class of 2010, included gap year alongside workforce, military and "undecided"—but for now it's only a micro-trend.

At William Jewell College in Liberty, Kan. for instance, typically just one or two of each year's 300 freshmen ask to defer their first year, and those requests aren't always gap-related.

Not everyone agrees on what a gap year is or when it's taken. Generally it's the year after high school. But some college graduates, rather than dive into grad school or the job market, do a gap year first.

A year that bridges secondary school and university is now more common in places like Great Britain.

Good for the Right Kind of Student

"A gap year, for some students, is a really great idea," says Rick Winslow, vice president for enrollment and student affairs at Jewell.

It's a decision that young people need to make with their parents, Winslow says. For students who are "developmentally mature enough to take a year off and focus on something they're passionate about," it can be a success, he says. A political science major at Jewell took a gap year before his junior year of college to work on political campaigns and travel internationally.

But "for students who are just blowing in the breeze and not sure what they want to do with the rest of their life, a gap year can be a waste of time," Winslow says.

"I'm worried - he says he's having a 'staycation' for his gap year."

"I'm worried, he says he's having a 'staycation' for his gap year." Cartoon by Richard Jolley/www.CartoonStock.com © Richard Jolley. Reproduction rights obtainable from www.CartoonStock.com.

Plenty of Options

For students (and parents) who like the idea of a gap year, there are no lack of alternatives. Books like *The Complete Guide to the Gap Year. The Best Things to Do Between High School and College* list page after page of programs.

A gap year can be spent in volunteer service (AmeriCorps, Habitat for Humanity and others) here or abroad. There are cultural immersion programs such as Adventure Ireland and the Southern France Youth Institute Plus programs focused on adventure, language study, the outdoors, sports, even sailing.

The cost can vary widely. AmeriCorps gives members an allowance for living expenses and $5,350 to be put toward college. Programs sometimes provide housing and food. Scholarships

Many US students spend a gap year volunteering for organizations such as Habitat for Humanity (pictured) or Americorps.

are available for some gap year programs. But gap students typically have to pay to do volunteer work.

A gap year might end up costing just as much as, or more than, college.

Life Experience

Which brings us back to Grant Stauffer, who will spend what would have been his first semester of college at the National Outdoor Leadership School. NOLS for short. For three months he'll be backpacking, rock-climbing, back country skiing and more across the Western U.S. while learning leadership and how to work with others. He'll be in a gap program for students his age. He'll earn 16 credit hours toward college.

Next spring, he'll take some classes at Johnson County Community College. Then a year from now, he plans to enter Colorado State University as a sophomore.

"Every time I talk to someone who's already gone through college, 75 percent of them say, 'I wish I'd done something like that,'" Stauffer says. "I think it tends to be the people who change majors midway through college."

His mom, Sara Stauffer of Prairie Village, describes Grant as the most "wet cement" of her three sons. She and husband Ward were afraid he'd end up taking five or six years to earn a degree.

"For us, the college credit (through NOLS) wasn't as important as the life experience and growing up and learning a little more about himself and doing something positive," Sara says.

The idea of taking a year off used to be seen like "that 'Failure to Launch' feeling instead of a positive life experience," she adds. But a pre-college break can be similar to a semester or year spent studying abroad, "but you end up doing it on the front end," she says.

A Gap Year Abroad

Which is just what Annie Wake, a 2008 high school grad, did. She repeated her senior year in the small country town of Andenne, Belgium, through a Rotary International program. She lived with three host families there. She'd spent three weeks in France between her sophomore and junior years, also a Rotary program, so she and her parents had some idea of what to expect.

In Belgium, "half my battle for the first few months was understanding what was on the board," Wake says. The handwriting, the way numbers were written, were strange to her.

"And that's what's exciting about going abroad. You come up against these challenges you weren't really expecting."

Then last fall [2009] she started at DePauw University in Greencastle, Ind. A student manning an orientation booth told her later that she looked different—more confident, independent—than other first-year students.

Which was true, Wake says.

"I definitely didn't feel as homesick as other students, because eight hours (from her family's home) doesn't really compare to a seven-hour time difference."

New Directions

Jenny Sander's gap year experience was also overseas—in Israel—but with an unexpected conclusion. The 2006 high school grad thought she had her future mapped out pre-med, med school, "that whole track."

But first came the gap year, a program called Nativ, sponsored by United Synagogue of Conservative Judaism. She spent the fall of 2006 studying at a university in Jerusalem, taking field trips to such locales as the West Bank and even getting "a little taste of the army" in a week spent with Israel Defense Forces. She and 85 other young people lived in a hostel.

The second semester, she lived in the desert city of Be'er Sheva volunteering at a special needs preschool.

After that year she entered Washington University in St. Louis. About a year and a half in, Sander decided she did not want to go to medical school.

Her year in Israel made her realize "there's a whole lot more out there than what I always thought I wanted to do," she says. Her new major is international studies with a minor in women and gender studies. Now a senior, she's thinking about careers in social work or public health.

Jeff Anderson, a counselor at Johnson County Community College, says a lot of students "probably position themselves better by choosing to step out and take some time off.

"They seem to be more focused and in some cases more motivated, and (often) they're making some sacrifice to be back in school again. They have a different approach than someone who's right out of high school."

SIXTEEN

College Is Not the Only Option

Suzanne Lucas

In the following viewpoint, Suzanne Lucas makes the argument that, depending on students' skills, talents, and career aspirations, college might not be the best choice for them. She points out that many satisfying careers do not require a college education—and that, in fact, these careers can often be more lucrative in the long run. She advocates that students think about noncollege paths not as failures or as disappointments but as alternate routes to the American dream. Lucas has been a human resources professional for close to a decade.

I know all about the American dream, because in college I read *The Great Gatsby* for three different classes. (See, I've already proven the point of my headline, because how often have I used that knowledge in life after college?)

There are two types of jobs in this world: jobs where you shower before going, and jobs where you shower after you get home. Somewhere along the line we decided that the former were "good" jobs and the latter were "bad" jobs. High schools started pushing everyone into college-prep classes and suddenly, we're living in a world devoid of plumbers. But when a pipe bursts in our basement and begins spewing water all over our

Students who opt out of college can find promising careers in skilled trade jobs, such as plumbing.

piles of clothes that we promised ourselves we'll fit into again someday, we can discuss how it makes us feel with the proper angst and punctuation.

An Expensive Trade-Off

Mike Rowe, the host of the TV show *Dirty Jobs*, was in Washington last week [2010] to discuss the non-college path. *The Washington Examiner* reported:

> "I don't think the country is going to fall back in love with manufacturing, and I don't think these policies are going to change, until or unless we reignite a fundamental relationship with dirt, work, and the business of making things, as opposed to the business of buying them," Rowe said.

> He said one of the reasons this is occurring is because community colleges and vocational education have taken the backseat to four-year college degrees.

> "It's not happening because people hate community colleges, it's not happening because people hate the trades, it's happening because we're promoting a very specific kind of education at the expense of the others," he said.

Different Intelligences

Think about it for a minute. It you have talents that include manual dexterity and the desire not to be micro-managed, to set your own hours, or to just not sit in a cube all day, there are some "dirty jobs" that might be right up your alley. They're more plentiful than most desk jobs, they often pay better, and you won't have onerous student loans getting between you and your dream house (or boat or ski cabin, or whatever it is you dream about).

On Glenn Reynolds's blog Instapundit, a plumber reported the following:

> I am a very smart woman from a book-smart but not blue-collar family and I am a plumber. I sought this job out about five years ago, and I think that I love my job more

than almost anyone I know. I need a combination of mechanical intelligence (Obvious), social intelligence (you have to communicate with customers), and independence (I am an employee of a medium-sized company but am on my own in the field (though I can call if I run into trouble)). I know that there is not an infinite demand for everyone in the U.S. to repair their neighbors house problems but [dang], the high efficiency natural gas boilers come with computer controls and a 100 page manual. No-one should be ashamed to be the one who can come and make someone's life better (If my grammar or spelling is off, I never claimed to have verbal intelligence.)

Best-Paying Blue-Collar Jobs, 2010

Job Title	Annual Salary
Elevator installer and repairer	$67,950
Powerhouse substation and relay repairer	$61,700
Transportation inspector	$61,110
Oil and gas rotary drill operator	$59,560
Commercial diver	$58,060
Petroleum pump system operator	$56,990
Boilermaker	$56,680
Electrical power line installer and repairer	$58,860
Locomotive engineer	$53,590
Telecommunications equipment installer	$52,990

Taken from: Susan Adams, "America's Best-Paying Blue-Collar Jobs," Forbes.com, June 6, 2010. www.forbes.com/2010/06/11/high-paying-blue-collar-leadership-careers-jobs.html.

Something for Everyone

A technical-school instructor blogs that enrollment at his school is up. He argues:

> My school (three campuses) serves an entire county, and sixteen sending schools [high schools from which a college draws students], with career education. The $8,000 it costs to give a high school senior nine months of training with us is hands down the best value in education available. Our "product," a technical education, stands shoulder to shoulder with post secondary education costing $40,000 per class seat per year. I know this, as I serve on an industry team that evaluates these schools for certification.

Of course, technical schools and blue collar work aren't for everyone. But, neither are a university degree and the cube life that follows. If you're after the American dream, don't forget to look at an alternative path. It can get you there as well.

What You Should Know About Choosing a College

Facts About US Colleges and Students

According to the National Center for Education Statistics at the US Department of Education:

- In 2009 enrollment at degree-granting institutions reached 20,428,000; male students totaled 8,770,000; and female students totaled 11,658,000.
- Of those students enrolled in degree-granting institutions in 2009:
  - 62.3% were white;
  - 14.3% were black;
  - 12.5% were Hispanic;
  - 6.5% were Asian/Pacific Islander; and
  - 1% were American Indian/Alaska Native.
- Of the 1,601,000 bachelor's degrees conferred in 2008–2009, the most popular majors were:
  - business (348,000);
  - social sciences and history (169,000);
  - health sciences (120,000); and
  - education (102,000).

Costs and Financial Aid

According to the National Center for Education Statistics:

- Total tuition and room and board rates charged for full-time undergraduate students averaged $21,189 per year for four-year institutions in the 2009–2010 school year. In public institutions, that average was $15,014; in private institutions, the average was $32,790.

- In 2007–2008, 66 percent of all undergraduates received some type (or types) of financial aid; for those who received any aid, the total average amount received was $9,100:
  - 52 percent received grants averaging $4,900;
  - 38 percent took out an average of $7,100 in student loans;
  - 7 percent received aid through work-study jobs averaging $2,400 in wages;
  - 2 percent received an average of $5,400 in veterans' benefits; and
  - 4 percent had parents who took out an average of $10,800 in Parent PLUS loans (Parent Loans for Undergraduate Students).

Tools to Identify Your Interests and Aptitudes

- The Myers-Briggs Type Indicator is a personality inventory that may help clarify appropriate occupations and associated academic majors. Many unofficial versions are available to take for free online, including post-inventory analysis.
- The Strong Interest Inventory is a questionnaire that gauges interest in a variety of topics and fields. It is available from school guidance counselors.
- The Armed Services Vocational Aptitude Battery is a series of tests that gauges skills in areas including arithmetical reasoning, word knowledge, paragraph comprehension, and mechanical comprehension. It is available through guidance counselors and has broader utility than just entry into the armed services.
- The *Occupational Outlook Handbook* is a survey of preparation, job prospects, and associated duties of many different careers. It is available through a school or public library.

Admission Exams to Take

Different schools require different entrance exams; some require specific exams while others accept multiple exams.

- SAT (tests math, vocabulary, and reading comprehension)
- ACT (tests English, math, reading, and science)
- TOEFL (tests English proficiency for nonnative speakers)

Understanding Early Decision

"Early decision" and "early action" are confusing terms that you might hear. Early decision is an option that can be exercised if you have a clear top college choice. If you plan to apply for early decision, you apply to a single school early in your senior year and receive a decision by December. If you are accepted, you are obligated to enroll at the school, regardless of other factors such as scholarships or financial aid. Early action has similar timelines but is not binding; early action applications often allow students to apply to more than one school using this method. Either way, early decision or early action applications can help students who have a clear vision of their top choice alleviate much of the pressure of the senior year of high school.

Criteria to Use When Evaluating Colleges

- Evaluate the **location,** including distance from home and ease of visiting family; whether the campus is in a rural or urban environment; the climate of the region; and crime statistics in the area.
- Consider the **type of school** you are looking for: private vs. public; coed vs. single-sex student body; whether a school has a religious affiliation; whether a college or university has a particular academic focus such as environmental education, experiential education, or a specialty in science and technology.
- Considerations of **size** include the student body population as well as the geographic size of the campus.
- **Admission requirements** vary by school. Be sure you understand application deadlines, accepted entrance exams, national college ranking, average GPA, and the school's acceptance rate.
- Do not forget about **financial aid,** including deadlines, required forms, and the types and amount of aid offered.

- Understand the college's **housing** options, including the availability and location of dorms for first-year students and upperclassmen, the proximity and affordability of any off-campus housing, options for commuting students, and availability and flexibility of dining plans.
- Visit and evaluate **facilities**, including academic facilities such as classrooms, libraries, and labs as well as recreational facilities such as fitness complexes and student centers.
- Ask about campus **activities** such as clubs, a Greek system, and athletics, both varsity and intramural.
- **Academics** are important, of course. Be sure to find out whether a college is accredited. Survey what majors the college offers and ask about its student-faculty ratio, class sizes, and opportunities to study abroad.
- Whether or not financial aid is an option, **college expenses** are an important piece of the equation. Knowing about current costs and recent trends regarding tuition, room/board, fees, and books can help you project the kinds of costs you can expect.

What College Admissions Officers Look For

According to admissions coach Paul Hemphill, college admissions officers today are looking for more than the traditionally "well-rounded" student. Some of the most important attributes admissions committees at selective colleges are looking for are:

- specialization in one extracurricular activity;
- excelling in that activity;
- demonstrations of leadership;
- class choices;
- good grades;
- good test scores;
- letters of recommendation; and
- evidence of passion and commitment.

What You Should Do About Choosing a College

Start Early

Many experts, both high school guidance counselors and college admissions officers, advise getting started with the college search process in ninth grade. Chances are you won't be ready to start visiting colleges yet; you probably do not even have a clear idea of what you are looking for. But that is what this time is for—to start asking questions, exploring subjects, and learning as much as you can about different types of colleges and which ones might fit your needs. Meet with your guidance counselor to talk about college prep courses, take questionnaires such as the Strong Interest Inventory, and make a plan for your high school coursework.

Outside of school, talk with older friends or relatives who have gone through the college search process recently. Ask questions: What was their experience like? What would they have done differently? What advice would they have for you? You might even want to start organizing a college binder to document your search and explorations.

Get Organized

The website for the Student Loan Marketing Association, a student loan provider referred to informally as Sallie Mae, notes that "organization is the key to a successful school search." As soon as you take college entrance exams, you will start receiving lots of information from many different schools. Sallie Mae suggests taking a few straightforward steps to construct an organized college search and avoid becoming overwhelmed by all the information you'll be gathering:

Create a filing system. This can be a filing cabinet, basket, or even a drawer, something that can hold many folders. You will want a separate file folder for each school. In the folder, collect everything relevant to that school: application materials, brochures, interview questions, scholarship materials, etc.

Gather supplies. Sallie Mae suggests other supplies that can help you organize your materials: markers, Post-it notes, résumé paper, envelopes, and postage stamps.

Keep a calendar. Whether you keep it online or on paper, keep a single calendar that notes all your application, scholarship, and financial aid deadlines, school visits, and other key dates.

Create contact lists. Collect names, phone numbers, and addresses for key personnel at each of the schools you visit. Also keep track of contact information for the people who serve as your references.

Evaluate your schools. Periodically evaluate your top schools based on the criteria that are important to you. Use a standard worksheet for each top contender, and keep the completed worksheets in each school's folder for easy reference.

Visit Schools

Although most school visits will take place during your junior and senior years in high school, it is not a bad idea to start earlier if you are interested in the fact-finding portion of the search process. Try visiting colleges in or near your hometown, even if you do not think those schools are prospects for you. Doing so will expose you to different types of schools and help you clarify what factors are important to you. Later, when you have narrowed down the types of schools that interest you, make a point of visiting colleges on your short list—and while you are at it, visit other schools in the same vicinity. Seeing several colleges in a single week can be overwhelming, so be sure to keep good notes and add them to the organizational system you have developed. Time your visits when the colleges will be in session, so that you can see what the school is really like for current students. Call ahead to make appointments with admissions counselors and to make arrangements to visit classes, take tours, eat in the dining hall, and even stay overnight in a dorm room. Visiting colleges is the best possible way to gauge a school's environment and to test your own "fit" with their campus, culture, and other students. Visiting plenty of schools can help you clarify your own college preferences. Visit your top contenders more than once, if you can.

Know Your Deadlines

If you have set up a good organizational system, sticking to deadlines should be easy. There is a lot to keep track of, though—everything from the dates for entrance exams such as the SAT and ACT, to application deadlines for schools, to interview dates and scholarship weekends, to financial aid and scholarship application deadlines, to the all-important notification dates, when you will find out whether you are in, out, or wait-listed.

Get Help

Today, there are so many resources available to potential college applicants, there is no reason not to take advantage of these tools and resources. These can include in-person resources such as your high school guidance counselor, private admissions consultants, test-taking courses, college alumni networks, family, and friends. Do not overlook your high school and public library, where there are many reference books and magazines that collect key facts and ratings of schools in a single volume. Finally, the Internet is a treasure trove of resources, including college and university websites, online ratings, and even resource sites that help you organize your own search and evaluate your choices.

Apply for Financial Aid

Even if you think you will not qualify for need-based federal student aid, have your family fill out the Free Application for Federal Student Aid, or FAFSA. Submitting the form may be a requirement for other, merit-based scholarships, as well as for programs such as federal work-study and other on-campus jobs. The forms are detailed and time-consuming, but they can pay off in unexpected ways.

Relax and Enjoy

The college search can be stressful, but if you approach it in a more relaxed and organized way, it can actually be a fun and exciting exploration of the next phase in your life. Taking your time and approaching the process carefully and confidently will help you make the most of the whole experience—and maybe even have time to enjoy your high school career.

ORGANIZATIONS TO CONTACT

The editors have compiled the following list of organizations concerned with the issues debated in this book. The descriptions are derived from materials provided by the organizations. All have publications or information available for interested readers. The list was compiled on the date of publication of the present volume; names, addresses, phone and fax numbers, and e-mail and Internet addresses may change. Be aware that many organizations take several weeks or longer to respond to inquiries, so allow as much time as possible.

Adventures in Education (AIE)
PO Box 83100
Round Rock, TX 78683-3100
website: www.aie.org

The AIE is a public service site sponsored by the Texas Guaranteed Student Loan Corporation. It offers users a number of resources on choosing a college and paying for education, as well as guidance on career choice and financial planning. The organization distributes the free weekly e-newsletter *AIEmail* that offers students and families up-to-date information on deadlines, events, news, and advice.

American Association of Community Colleges (AACC)
One Dupont Circle NW, Washington, DC 20036
(202) 728-0200
fax: (202) 833-2467
website: www.aacc.nche.edu

The AACC was founded in 1920 and has since become the national "voice for community colleges." In addition to providing professional resources for its twelve-hundred-member organizations, the association's website also offers students and parents important planning tools. These include a Community College Finder, fact sheets about community colleges, information on funding, and lists of notable community college alumni.

A Better Chance
253 W. Thirty-Fifth St., 6th Fl., New York, NY 10001
(646) 346-1310
fax: (646) 346-1311
e-mail: stimmons@abetterchance.org
website: www.abetterchance.org

Founded in 1963, A Better Chance operates with the goal of improving lifelong educational and career outcomes for students of color by increasing their access to high-quality secondary schools. The nonprofit organization partners with private schools to generate scholarships for young people of color, and approximately 96 percent of the students helped by the organization enroll in college immediately after graduating from high school.

The College Board
45 Columbus Ave., New York, NY 10023-6992
(212) 713-8000
website: www.collegeboard.org

Best known for developing the SAT college entrance exam, the College Board is a nonprofit membership organization made up of nearly six thousand educational institutions. In addition to its numerous testing programs, the College Board offers tools and advocacy for students planning for college and seeking financial aid. Its website offers numerous tools for students on finding, planning for, and applying to colleges, as well as information on scholarships and loans. It also provides tips and tools for study skills and test preparation.

College Forward
PO Box 142308, Austin, TX 78714
(512) 452-4800
fax: (512) 452-4848
website: www.collegeforward.org

College Forward provides college planning assistance to economically disadvantaged young people. Participating students receive one-on-one assistance during the entire college application and financial aid process.

College Planning Network
43 Bentley Pl., Port Townsend, WA 98368
(206) 323-0624
e-mail: seacpn@collegeplan.org
website: www.collegeplan.org

The College Planning Network serves primarily students in the Pacific Northwest, but its resources are relevant to students everywhere. Its website offers resources and tips for students as early as elementary school, as well as for adults returning to college. The network offers workshops on financial aid for college.

Independent Educational Consultants Association (IECA)
325 Old Lee Hwy., Ste. 510, Fairfax, VA 22030
(703) 591-4850
fax: (703) 591-4860
e-mail: info@iecaonline.com
website: www.iecaonline.com

The IECA is a professional organization for college consultants. Its website offers students and parents guidance on how to find an educational consultant, questions to ask when interviewing a consultant, and how to make the most of the college consulting process.

US Federal Student Aid
website: www.college.gov

This site provided by the United States government is a gateway to resources for prospective and current college students. It offers numerous links to topics such as college choice, federal student grant programs, and federal student loans.

BIBLIOGRAPHY

Books

Donald Asher, *Cool Colleges: For the Hyper-Intelligent, Self-Directed, Late Blooming, and Just Plain Different.* Berkeley, CA: Ten Speed, 2007.

Howard Bartee Jr., *The Next Level: Six Perspectives on the College Choice Process of Student Athletes.* Seattle: CreateSpace, 2011.

Andrew Ferguson, *Crazy U: One Dad's Crash Course on Getting His Kid into College.* New York: Simon & Schuster, 2011.

Michele A. Hernandez, *A Is for Admission: The Insider's Guide to Getting into the Ivy League and Other Top Colleges.* New York: Grand Central, 2011.

Lillian Luterman, *In! College Admissions and Beyond.* New York: Abbeville, 2011.

Katie Malachuk, *You're Accepted: Lose the Stress. Discover Yourself. Get into the College That's Right for You.* New York: Kaplan, 2009.

Robin Mamlet, *College Admission: From Application to Acceptance, Step by Step.* New York: Three Rivers, 2011.

Dave Marcus, *Acceptance: A Legendary Guidance Counselor Helps Seven Kids Find the Right Colleges—and Find Themselves.* New York: Penguin, 2009.

Carl Mecklenburg, *Heart of a Student Athlete: All-Pro Advice for Competitors and Their Families.* Virginia Beach, VA: Bernard, 2009.

Cal Newport, *How to Be a High School Superstar: A Revolutionary Plan to Get into College by Standing Out (Without Burning Out).* New York: Three Rivers, 2010.

Robert J. Sternberg, *College Admissions for the 21st Century.* Cambridge, MA: Harvard University Press, 2010.

Periodicals and Internet Sources

Jenny Anderson, "For a Standout College Essay, Applicants Fill Their Summers," *New York Times*, August 5, 2011.

Kim Clark, "The Challenge for Black Colleges," *US News & World Report*, September 1, 2009.

Nick Clunn, "Your College Choice Virtually in Your Hand," *Seattle Post-Intelligencer*, October 14, 2010.

Josh Dehaas, "Where Do I Belong?," *Maclean's Guide to Canadian Universities*, 2011.

Francesca Di Meglio, "College: How to Decide," *Business Week*, April 28, 2008.

Howard Fineman, "One Family's Road Trip," *Newsweek*, August 20, 2007.

Neal Gabler, "The College Admissions Scam," *Boston Globe*, January 10, 2010.

Thomas K. Grose, "Taking a Page from Britain," *US News & World Report*, September 1, 2009.

Kathleen Kingsbury, "Dirty Secrets of College Admissions," *Daily Beast*, January 9, 2009. www.thedailybeast.com/articles/2009/01/09/dirty-secrets-of-college-admissions.html.

Ron Lieber, "Balancing Debt Against College Choice," *New York Times*, March 23, 2011.

Jay Mathews, "Finding the Right College for You," *Newsweek*, August 17, 2009.

Tovia Smith, "Behind the Scenes: How Do You Get into Amherst?," National Public Radio, March 28, 2011. www.npr.org/npr/134916924/Amherst-Admissions-Process.

Mark Starr, "From Cow Pasture to Campus," *Newsweek*, August 17, 2009.

Jacques Steinberg, "Don't Worry, Be Students," *New York Times Magazine*, September 30, 2007.

INDEX

PICTURE CREDITS